Reality - the quality or state of being real.

reality. (2008). In *Merriam-Webster Online Dictionary*.

http://www.merriam-webster.com/dictionary/reality

What is YOUR reality?

Notes

Fishing for Reality

Catching Helpful Ideas That WILL Make a Difference for YOU

Published by Lightning Source International
www.lightningsource.com

Copyright © PWPDA (Paul White Personal Development and Associates) 2008

All rights reserved worldwide. No part of this book may be reproduced or transmitted in any form or by any means, electronic or otherwise, including photocopying, or by any information storage and retrieval system, without the written permission of the publisher and/or PWPDA (except where permitted by law).

The author of this book does not dispense medical advice or prescribe the use of any technique as a form of treatment for medical problems. The intent of the author is to offer information of a general nature to help you in your quest for well-being. In the event you use any of the information in this book for yourself, which is your constitutional right, the author and publisher assume no responsibility for your actions.

Cover Photo: *Skipper* Michael Joseph Bruce pointing the way – "Straight Ahead!"

ISBN: 978-0-9810547-0-4

Dedication

This *Doctor of Life* (L.D.) project is a reflection of all my life experiences. This book, however, is a direct result of my collection of life teachings and wisdom from a man who cannot be described merely with words. All who came in contact with him, especially small children and strangers, were instantly attracted and dazzled by his persona. Many of the kids unrelated to our family also called him "Poppy Bruce" in a very short time. He really was a fisher and a life teacher whose presence amazed those who came to know him. At environmental community meetings, in his later years, Poppy Bruce was noted as the one to patiently sit and listen. When he had something to say, however, he said it. All in attendance, knowing that Poppy Bruce could see the bigger picture, took his wisdom and words to heart.

Gifted with far greater knowledge than any university professor I have ever experienced and filled with more wisdom than any multimillionaire I have ever encountered, he understood the ways and means of living a full and happy life. He passed away a few months before his 88th birthday. It was speculated that he lived with cancer for over two decades, and in my estimation, the cancer was probably in his body longer than anyone will ever know. How did he survive and thrive for so long? Only one word comes to mind: **attitude**. "Skipper" Michael Joseph Bruce had the attitude of a successful champion - one hundred percent all the way. I can still see him smiling and leading the way as we walked through the woods to get to our fishing destination. After a long day with Mother Nature, he, knowing that we were home free, would kiss the car.

Today, in a higher place, we can be sure he is "Frisky and still fishing."

Being a *Doctor of Life*, Poppy Bruce not only talked about positive thinking ideas and life success strategies, he lived them. Many talk the talk; he walked the walk. Poppy Bruce's examples, life philosophies and wisdom are too valuable not to be shared. I am thankful to be able to share these with you. Words are powerful indeed, and Poppy Bruce, a master wordsmith, knew how to use them well. His words, spoken at the right time, not only helped him but also, helped those who were lucky enough to be influenced by him. Thank you Poppy Bruce, one more time, for everything. Going to visit you and Nan for card games and lunches with the fresh smell of home-made bread baking will ever remind me of the things that truly matter. Coming to the door and waving good-bye, as you did on many occasions when I departed, still brings tears to my eyes. You and Nan were right: I did eventually "get one" and, more importantly, I learned how to help others "get one", too. Poppy Bruce, you really are the greatest catch ... ever.

Fishing for Reality:
Catching Helpful Ideas That Will Make a Difference for YOU

Contents

Dedication	5
Contents	7
Dear Reader	9
Introduction	13
1. Hooked … on New Beginnings	23
2. It's MY Fault!	37
3. On the Rocks	53
4. The Way to a Man's Heart…	67
5. Yes Man, Yes Maam!	79
6. The First 2 P's Life Leadership	91
7. The Final 2 P's Life Leadership	107
8. Majoring in MAJOR Life Areas	125
9. Health is Wealth and MUCH MORE!	139
10. Onward We Sail	153
Concluding Story – Charmed and Ready for Action!	163
Acknowledgements	169
About the Author	175

Dear Reader,

Fishing for Reality is for all lifelong learners in search of more meaning, more joy, more truth and more ideas to live life to the fullest. It is a look at reality. Let us call it my L.D. dissertation, for it has been, and will continue to be, a work in progress. This book is, I feel, an expression of the ideas and virtues which are essential for one to acquire a "Doctor of Life."

Anything in life can be accomplished. The secret is to have a solid foundation of ideas upon which to build your future. The ideas contained within *Fishing for Reality* have been adopted and refined for you because it is often easier to get started with some help. My educational foundation is, of course, a result of my studies. More significantly, however, my life foundation comes from my original mentor, "Skipper" Michael Joseph Bruce, an extraordinary individual whose knowledge and wisdom about the things that really matter linger with me still.

Like many students today, I left university - lost. I had plenty of education and some work experience, in teaching, in psychology, in health and in physical education; however, I was not challenged enough to reach my full potential. I, therefore, returned to the basics - basic ideas waiting to be put to work. When you work the ideas, the ideas work for you. These basic ideas are not new. They have been handed down through the ages and are fundamental in life's journey.

You do not need letters after your name to make a difference in society. Through the whole process of collecting ideas and studying the top world and community successes, I have come to reaffirm that your own personal development process is what matters most. You need ideas put to work to challenge you to challenge yourself. You will find the ideas presented here useful, and I am certain that if you want life change to occur, using these lifelong learning ideas will help start that process.

Enjoy,

Paul

*The greatest tragedy
Is to spend your whole life fishing,
Only to discover that
It was not fish you were after.*

Henry David Thoreau

Introduction

I had just finished reading Denis Waitley's book, *Seeds of Greatness,* when the thought hit me. The same "seeds of greatness" planted in Denis at a young age, "Skipper" Michael Joseph Bruce, my grandfather, planted in me. Poppy Bruce was a skipper on his father's schooner, *The James and Martha,* based out of Long Harbor, Placentia Bay, Newfoundland and Labrador, Canada. A "skipper", usually the one with the most experience and wisdom for decision making, is the leader or captain of a fishing vessel.

"The servant is not greater than the master", my Poppy Bruce, would say. He meant public servants, or public employees, and politicians are not greater than the ones who voted them to serve. If only our world had more admirable leaders and life teachers like Poppy Bruce. He learned well from his father, "Skipper" Jim (James Bruce), on the North Atlantic seas. My great-grandfather, Skipper Jim, was originally from Long Harbour, Placentia Bay. I remember my relatives and family friends talking about how Skipper Jim would influence the election vote in the whole community. Community members would gather around the wharf a week before the election to see who "they" were voting for when time came to cast the ballot. People in the fishing community trusted his wisdom and leadership ability in times of uncertainty.

Apparently my great-grandfather was also a speaker and a community leader in various ways. Poppy Bruce would tell me of times when his father, Skipper Jim, would have to go into a house in the community to break up a fight between parents of a young boy who would come running for help saying, "Jim! Jim! Dad is beating up Mom again - Help!" Skipper Jim would use his physical force and strength to restrain the man and stop him from further abusing his wife. We know this happens everywhere, but "How many Skipper Jim's are really out there in our communities and cities?" We need more.

Skipper Jim had no problems with helping out his fellow community members in times of trouble, often sharing what he had with anyone in need. He too, like Poppy Bruce, was a man to be admired in his simple teachings of life. Poppy Bruce would tell me how Skipper Jim told him to "Speak out" and practice your ultimate freedom here in the western world - your freedom of speech. Isn't our freedom of speech the most precious ultimate freedom? Why do we often fail to remember this? Why do we not practice it daily? Our fore-fathers gave their lives unselfishly in WWI and WWII so we could have freedom - freedom to win, freedom to lose, freedom to speak out and freedom to choose. In this 21st century of turmoil and constant change, it is something to ponder.

My grandfather (who will be called Skipper Bruce henceforth) was highly influenced by Mother Nature. An environmentalist, long before his time, Skipper Bruce predicted many things - the fishery collapse in many parts of the world, the globalization impact, technological change, world pollution, and the corrupting power of many politicians. As skipper on his father's schooner when his father retired from fishing, Skipper Bruce followed the wind, the moon, the seasons and the laws of nature to help him live an extraordinary life. His positive lessons of leading a full and happy life are valuable in today's world.

His approach to life was quite simple: be positive, be happy, never quit. He believed tough times make tough people. He believed in helping each other. He believed, of course, that experience is the best teacher. This was some of his simple, yet powerful philosophy for life. His life philosophy is one from which we all can learn, grow and move towards a better future. In times of complexity, simplicity is often the answer.

Skipper Bruce introduced me to fly-fishing when I was a young boy. We would go "trouting", as is referenced in Newfoundland culture, in the summer season. I remember the day when I asked him, "Who are all those people and why are they standing on the bridge?" Men of various ages and sizes, dressed in rain suits and fishing gear, were standing on the bridge where I would swim in another month when the temperature warmed up. The bridge was over the Northeast River just outside of my hometown, Dunville, Placentia Bay. We drove on the "old road" (it was not paved with asphalt) to our fishing destination as he pondered my question. His response to my life changing question came abruptly; "They are salmon anglers in pursuit of the king of the sea, the Atlantic salmon."

Skipper Bruce worked with his father as a commercial salmon fisherman in Long Harbour, Placentia Bay, when it was legal to fish with nets for Atlantic salmon. I remember Skipper Bruce telling me how his father would glaze the salmon in a large freezer for storage. With glazing, the fish was dipped in cold water and frozen, then dipped again and frozen, making several layers of ice on the fresh silvery fish. Skipper Bruce had some experience with "salmon fishing" but not hooking one on a fly rod (one of life's greatest challenges and most exhilarating thrills). My question on this day was probably the most important question I have ever asked anyone in my life. Within one week, I had Skipper Bruce convinced that we were going to pursue the Atlantic salmon as fly fishermen - a new adventure for him, and for me.

Being Skipper Bruce's sidekick, helper, and outdoor buddy, was a learning experience far greater than any formal training I have ever received. I was always with him to catch trout, both in the summer and in the winter, to pick blueberries and partridgeberries, and to snare rabbits in the fall and winter hunting seasons. We sometimes released a live rabbit out of our snare. He did this to get my reaction and teach me about life - to live and to let live. On one occasion, when I was ten years old, a released hare stopped, turned and faced us - thanking us for its freedom. Skipper Bruce valued, with dignity, all life forms.

When he retired, I also performed side jobs as his pipe-fitting assistant. Now, we had a completely new challenge - fly fishing for the king of the sea, the Atlantic salmon. Little did I know what I was getting into! A future of lifelong learning, triumphs and set backs, as well as, real meaning to the words "education" and "reality" was now destined for delivery…and destined to be put in writing.

Society needs another win…NOW! Technology was supposed to make life easier and it accomplished its goal. In that process, however, it has also made life more difficult. Some technology has separated people from love and the things that matter most to everyone. How many people are lost, wandering through life, thinking that more money, a better spouse or kids, or more time will make life more meaningful? We do not need more of anything. We only need more of who we are and what we are all about as individuals.

The goal of this book is to help you become a better leader in your own life. It is the point of view of a professional speaker, mental health counselor, teacher and guidance counselor, grandson, avid angler and protégé. I wrote it for several reasons. First of all, this book is a look at life, at real leadership and success reality from a variety of examples, primarily from Skipper Bruce, who taught me that everyday is a "good" day. Skipper Bruce's simple, yet powerful life philosophies, must be shared in our current world of need. Real leaders, it seems, are few in today's world of challenge and change. I wish everyone had the experience that I had - growing up with a solid mentor who knew how to teach and attract the things he wanted in life. I like the metaphor of "fishing" which really means "attracting". By reading, connecting to, and applying some of these ideas, it is my hope that you will also become a better leader in the life of your family, friends and business. *All leaders are readers* is an adage worth its weight in gold. Leadership will be covered in Skipper Bruce's examples. The real ship you are leading is you! Why not tap into your talents and abilities and lead a life of adventure and satisfaction?

The second reason for writing this book is that I want to practice what I have advocated to so many people. We have all heard many teachers and scholars "talk the talk" about taking the road less traveled, about chasing your dream and life passion, about doing what others only wish they would do and, of course, about making a difference in our world. I have decided that it is time to act and be an example of what I preach. I believe in chasing my passion, not my pension. I seldom read the newspaper or watch TV. It is loaded with negativity. In studying the top successful people in the world of family, health, and business, I have come to realize that many of them do not listen to the media. They all read and listen to "voices of value" and things that are helpful. If I wanted negativity, I could easily find a fair-weathered friend or relative to give me my dose of "good news". The time is now "to walk your talk". I hope you enjoy, and apply, these simple, yet profound ideas on our journey together.

The third and final reason for this book is the main one. This book is for all students of life. Many people are not interested in self-improvement. I, like you, have witnessed them in staff rooms, on job sites, in stores and at the local coffee shop complaining about everything, but doing nothing about it. This book could help revolutionize these people…if they were only ready. Many are not ready. Are you? *Fishing for Reality* is about YOU, the reader. My hope is that you will take the ideas and lessons in it and apply them to your own life, where possible, and also share them with others.

These ideas will help you achieve health and wealth. They also will improve your relationships, career, and life. May you find in this life project some simple ideas and ways of looking at things that you never were taught or even considered. My real schooling began when I left university and went to "figure it all out" in our new phenomenal world of change. Formal schooling is very important but, it is not enough in today's world of global competition. We need constant daily lifelong learning when formal schooling ends. Our education system provides us with the preliminary tools for life success. After this, it is our responsibility to take matters in our own hands and keep learning.

In our school systems, we label kids Learning Disabled. I know. Being a certified assessor and school counselor, I have done this. Are they really disabled? Am I artistic disabled because I cannot draw or paint effectively? What an interesting question to ask! Many in the "system" often ask, "What is wrong with little Johnny?" As a starting point, I suggest that they ask, "What is right with him?" A slight change in educational philosophy can help work wonders, especially for the sake of the student.

Some of the best results I have discovered in relation to financial success, which is easily measured (it is a number!), have come from students who fell through the cracks and went through the school of "hard knocks". Teachers, parents and fellow students often told these students that they would never amount to anything. I am confident that you can name a few personal friends who have experienced this. You, like I, have read some of the super success stories that relate to real life accomplishment with little formal education. It is incredible! There really is no direct relationship between academic formal success and life success – unless we believe it. Stay in school, of course, but also remain a student and continuously collect ideas as you sail through life.

Books are powerful! We never know the ideas for life change that can be acquired from reading valuable literature.

We all struggle to get through life the way we best know how and, at times, we all need help along the way. The time we can save on the ideas from another is a powerful concept. Sometimes we get it right. Many times we get it wrong. Learning from others' successes and set-backs is lifelong learning, at its best. I am an expert on one person only, me. We are all experts in our own lives and, living in a free society, we sometimes take this for granted. A book, such as this one, can be the foundational spark that ignites the fuel at the right moment in time for your towering inferno of change, continuous growth and development. My hope is that this book will start that process.

These ideas cannot solve all of your problems. No book can. Action is needed for you to help solve your life challenges, but these ideas can and will help. In this book, I hope you will see your challenges and future possibilities in a different light. An old high school teacher of mine once said, "Life is a collection of problems to be solved." He made the statement in a physics class when we were discussing the career of engineering. Then he went on to say that engineers are nothing more than problem solvers. Thus, we are all engineers of life, leading our ships in various directions. A ship cannot survive without an engineer.

For those of you who never had a Skipper Bruce, I hope these ideas are meaningful. By applying the ideas in your own life, you will make things happen. Enjoy this journey and, more importantly, enjoy your own.

1

Hooked ... on New Beginnings

Keep searching, keep seeking, keep fishing and you will find answers.
Skipper Michael Joseph Bruce

We are all searching. On a daily basis we are searching for more of the next life experience, a better relationship and improved health, more financial freedom and happiness, better friends and associates, and anything that we think will make us happy. The search seems never ending and happiness is a common thread for human beings. Yes, we are all searching…for something.

This fast-paced world of instant access and globalization has people online shopping, online dating, online counseling and online seeking new, better and improved living. The career and life search is a challenging phenomenon. In psychology these days, we say "dust off your childhood" to find a unique hidden inborn talent that you never knew existed. I recently heard one professional speaker say that the happiest in society are those who went back and found some of their buried childhood talents and put these to work to craft a life of success and fulfillment. It does not have to be a new career path, but it may be a hobby to pursue part time or an activity that matches your values. Imagine earning a living at something you enjoy and do extremely well! It makes sense, doesn't it?

Childhood and Youth Memoirs

Mother Nature offers a place of peace and tranquility, away from the hustle and bustle of everyday life. Those, who can relate, know what we mean by the term "the great outdoors." I have spoken to many retired individuals who claim that if they could do it all again, they would make more time for fun with nature, smelling the roses along the way. There is something to be said about Mother Nature, and childhood.

Amazingly we can remember childhood experiences when someone made us feel super special. With my father working on the United States Naval Base (Argentia, Newfoundland and Labrador) as a civilian, and my mother a stay-at-home Mom helping to raise my brother and me, I was the perfect protégé for "Mr. Mike", as many of the locals called him.

Skipper Bruce was one of these extraordinary human beings who could "hook" anyone on his solid presence, dazzling personality, charisma, leadership and unusual kindness. As a young boy of about five or six years old, I remember driving with him in his green Dodge car, as he revved up the engine saying to the slow drivers, "COME ON! Drive it or park it! Get out of our way!" Of course, he did this for fun to impress me. I liked it when his voice rose as if he meant serious business. As safety was a major concept in his life philosophy I knew it was only for my amusement.

Seatbelt on, I could barely see over the dash. Away we went to our destination. There we were in the real classroom of life, learning about the things that matter most. I am certain that he learned, too, because he always commented that we learn best by experience and through teaching others. Those that teach, learn best. When we struggle to make something clear for another we help it make better sense for ourselves. Skipper Bruce was rarely, if ever, stuck for the right words at the right time in helping someone.

I vividly remember that day as if it were yesterday, when Skipper Bruce and I first decided to try fly-fishing for Atlantic salmon. Being only twelve years old, I was ready for action. While many of my friends in junior high school were wrapped up in their girlfriends and preliminary teenage temptation experiences, I was engrossed in my other classroom of learning with Mother Nature and, Skipper Bruce.

In some areas of the world, a fly-fishing angler can use bait, lures, and other contraptions to fish Atlantic salmon. In Newfoundland and Labrador where I grew up, it is "fly-fishing only", as a means of conservation. More importantly, I see it as the ultimate challenge, hooking and landing an often acrobatic Atlantic salmon on a fly rod. The Atlantic salmon is anadromous. As an adult it first spends its life in the ocean, feeding for survival and its journey ahead. When Mother Nature calls, it arrives in its river of origin to pass on the ultimate gift for future salmon generations. The Atlantic salmon lives in fresh and salt (sea) water during its life cycle, a unique combination for a life species.

During those early years of fly-fishing adventures, many changes were happening in the salmon fishery in Newfoundland and Labrador, Canada. Conservation measures were implemented and pressed on everyone to help prevent future extinction of the Atlantic salmon stocks. Simultaneously, Mother Nature had her own agenda. The rivers on the Avalon Peninsula of Newfoundland were often low and warm; often they were closed to fly-fishing. Nevertheless, I kept my positive attitude toward my new sport, as Skipper Bruce had told me to do so, especially after our first attempt at the new adventure.

The Northeast River just outside of my hometown, Dunville, was a raging flood on our opening day. We had our fly rods, salmon licenses, leader material to attach fly to fly line and, of course, our new selection of artificial Atlantic salmon flies. Skipper Bruce took me to fish a section of the river where many youth, including me, would swim in the summertime. There was a huge cliff on the other side of the river with trees overhanging, having been washed out from the torrential rain. I remember swimming there as a teenager, doing jumps, belly flops and dives off the main rock. On this day though, we meant business - fishing business that is.

When we got to the river it was evident that Mother Nature had been at work because the river was extremely high and there were many tributaries. Here salmon could swim more easily. Oftentimes fish take the path of least resistance. This is a life philosophy applicable to us all on occasion: when you must, take the path of least resistance.

Be Safe, Be Ready!

Skipper Bruce decided to put me on one path of least resistance, a tributary near the shore that looked like a perfect spot through which fish could swim. It was safe for me to stand on the rocks instead of having to wade out into the turbulent current of the "weedy hole" as we used to incorrectly call it. (The "weedy hole" is actually another pool further up the river.) Skipper Bruce was very safety conscious in everything that he did. "Always be safe," he would say, "Because safety must be a top priority in life." How right he was in times when companies placed profits above employee safety. Many times the employees lived in fear and did not stand up for themselves, thus making unsafe decisions. Far too often, we see people make careless decisions costing them too much, sometimes the ultimate cost - life itself. "Work hard, play hard, but, be safe" was a major component of Skipper Bruce's daily philosophy.

I stepped up near the river and was ready to cast my fly. I remember the fly well. It was a "thunder and lightning" pattern that we bought at the local drug store in Placentia. It was a #6 hook, average size for Atlantic salmon, containing a moose hair wing, black body with a gold tinsel rib, a yellow tail and a combination of blue and orange feather fibers for the underside wing commonly called a "throat."

Having ensured my safety on the river bank, Skipper Bruce proceeded to fish the major river stem in the main pool. As a new salmon angler, I was not efficient at casting the fly across the current. Through years of experience, I have now learned that presentation is the most important part of Atlantic salmon fishing, unlike fly-fishing for trout, where presentation is usually not as important as the fly you are casting. Trout take the fly for hunger or territorial purposes. Some of my fishing colleagues refer to trout as "dumb fish". I disagree. No fish, like no human being, can be labeled "dumb." No one really knows, however, why the Atlantic salmon rises to the river surface to take an artificial fly. It is part of the mystery of life itself, but one can speculate that "fishy" instinct underlies this tendency.

After six or eight casts in this flow of fresh water, my rod bent over like I had hooked into a Boeing 747, and my reel started to sing like a chainsaw on overdrive! **ZZZZZZZZZZzzzzzzzzzzz!!!** I was looking away as this happened but my focus immediately shifted back to the splashing and jumping in front of me. The fresh silvery torpedo had taken my fly unexpectedly and it proceeded to muscle down the river as if shot from a cannon! Before I had a chance to yell to Skipper Bruce, he was rushing over to see what the commotion was. The fish made one final springing leap and the fly line and leader came back and hit me in the face. Fish #1 was gone, just like that! As a rookie angler, I did not have time to lift my fly rod when the hook was set. It was both upsetting and startling. What a rush!

That first presentation was, no doubt, a fluke. Whatever I did to attract that fish it worked. What excitement to have the feel of a leaping Atlantic salmon on the end of your rod, solidly hooked and fighting to be free! Skipper Bruce estimated it to be seven or eight pounds, a far cry from the "big" half pound trout that we sometimes angled; and a far cry from the small pan-size "sardine trout" that my brother and father often brought home. That day I was "hooked" to a new activity that has taught me so much about life itself and all the twists and turns we each face on a daily basis. Do you have such an activity that has changed your life? Now is the perfect time to get hooked.

New Beginnings

That very first day on the river is still glowing like a beacon in my mind. It was a new beginning, a rise to meet a new challenge. It was also the beginning of a life passion and school of learning that many people use in their search for the meaning of it all. We all go through new beginnings in life on a daily basis. Each day is a new beginning in that we awake to a fresh new start, moving past yesterday while thinking about tomorrow and living for today. Some people break out of old relationships and enter new ones while other people begin new jobs, new careers and new adventures. What new beginnings have influenced you lately?

New beginnings can be quite challenging. Breaking free from the old to explore and pursue the new has halted many great ideas from hatching into tangible results. The best place to begin is "here" and "now" - the only place to begin. Many of us have suffered the guilt and shame from regrets of the past. Guilt and shame are deadly emotions that ultimately do not help us long term. These emotions must be acknowledged, but then released as we learn new ways of dealing with life and people. Change can be difficult, but it must be embraced.

Challenge and Change

One of the laws of physics tells us that a body in motion stays in motion, while an object at rest remains at rest. Thus, it takes more energy to start a new adventure than to maintain it. In the airline industry, it takes more fuel to get the plane off the ground than it does to keep it in the air for the duration of a three hour flight. Beginning something new, takes extra effort; however, it offers much lifelong learning. What idea have you been hooked on but cannot seem to make reality?

I have observed many rookie anglers begin fly-fishing for Atlantic salmon and then, for a variety of reasons, quit early in the game. More often than not their efforts were not rewarded because they did not persist and learn the correct techniques of fly-casting and presenting the fly properly in the river. In beginning a new business, for example, the common reality is that little or no profits will be generated during the first five to seven years. Despite what others may say and what statistics may reveal, many of these entrepreneurs, however, keep going and keep growing. The key, of course, is to change the approach until you get the result that you desire.

This is comparable to my first five years of fly-fishing for Atlantic salmon. "New", "young", "eager", "inexperienced", "enthusiastic" are words to describe the new angler. Like many, I was determined to become experienced and effective at fly-fishing. This did not happen overnight. In those first five years, I retained one fish! Wow! My father told me it was now costing about $12,500 per pound, for the fish that was eaten!!! I had to change or we could not afford to eat salmon!

The effort you put in will always equal the results you get out and many times the results obtained are multiplied, either positively or negatively depending on which seeds of effort you have planted. In beginning a new adventure, we often find ourselves putting in the extra hours and effort in anticipation of achieving results. In those early years of fly-fishing, I put in considerable hours with little or no results. There were trips to many different rivers in the province of Newfoundland and Labrador. Some people will wonder, as they always do, "Was it worth all the effort and energy expended?"

When you are hooked on something positive and can see the long term goal, it is worth the sweat, blood and tears up front. In the process, we never know what may happen along the way. So many people seek security today. In today's world of change, the only security is taking risks. Job security and life security are only ideas that keep people trapped. We must get out of the trap and get hooked. What has you "hooked" in life? It is time to get hooked on your passion! Do it for the right reasons, no matter what the critics and cynics want you to believe.

We all have unique passions in life. It has been said that "variety is the spice of life." If everyone did the same thing or looked the same way or had the same personality, imagine what a boring life it would be! What unique gifts and talents do you have? Discover your unique passions and go to work on these. Our talents and unique passions give meaning to life, not only for us but for others as well. As Abraham Maslow stated "Musicians must make music, artists must paint, poets must write, if they are to be ultimately at peace with themselves."

Growing Forward

No one grows up in a perfect environment. How can I make such a claim? It is simple. There is no perfection in life.

Here is a way to look at things: our parents did the best they could with what they had and knew at the time. Many of us fall into this category. Yes, things could have been better, but they could also have been much worse. Growing up in negative, dysfunctional environments is a common theme for many people I know and have worked with in counseling. What happens to one happens to all in some way. The past is not what determines how your future evolves. The determining piece in your future puzzle is YOU!

Ironically, many of the people who "come from nothing" eventually go forward and lead amazing lives of happiness and fulfillment. This is not taught in college or university; however, it is learned. The past is really a school of learning and has to be treated as such. Formal education is a necessary pre-requisite for career and life success. Hence, education is the key common denominator for everyone wanting more out of life. Life education, though, is what makes the real difference.

The Power of Teachers

As young children grow up, it is amazing how influential life teachers can be. What makes a good teacher? Can you remember your best teachers in school and in life? Some say that great teachers are made from their environments; others claim that they are born with the genetic influences to be great teachers. What a debate for university scholars! It does not really matter. Both are important. I remember having a conversation with a man who knew all the answers to life, had all the answers to world hunger and poverty, knew how to pick up and date the best looking women on the planet and was a self-proclaimed genius. He was a Ph.D. candidate in Mathematics at University and living on his Visa credit card. I thought to myself, "Not a person to have managing my new company!"

Favorable genes and tremendous life experiences certainly help contribute to being an extraordinary teacher. No matter whom the student was, Skipper Bruce was helpful, patient, and kind. I often thank my lucky stars for being influenced by such a positive role model. In his few years of fishing, he never did land an Atlantic salmon. Even though he only had the formal schooling of an elementary education because he went to work with his father on the North Atlantic seas at a young age, Skipper Bruce provided me with the foundational tools to use, not only for building an on-going successful fishing career, but also for building a life worth living. Thus, self education combined with a powerful mentor, teacher, or sensei, as is used in martial arts, can be what makes all the difference in the world for you.

Skipper Bruce often used examples and metaphors in his teaching. His communication skills were developed far beyond his acquired level of formal education. As a self-educated man he had this unique ability to teach in ways that only few people could possibly realize. Learning is a process and, oftentimes, a difficult process. Skipper Bruce's education philosophy was simple - we learn best from our mistakes.

Self-Forgiveness

One lesson that we all must learn is the lesson of self-forgiveness. Self-forgiveness is challenging. We are not programmed to act this way. Moving on and forgiving ourselves for the past negative experiences are necessary for self-development. We make mistakes and the best approach is to admit the mistake, forgive ourselves and move forward. In doing so, we open up the empowerment necessary for positive productive change. That first fish hooked and lost was an example of such a life experience. In the following years, Skipper Bruce often spoke of our very first day on the Northeast River and how he had tied a faulty knot in the line for this particular fishing situation. He found it very hard to forgive himself for such a mistake. We often find it difficult to forgive ourselves for some of our past mistakes. Have you ever felt this way? Many have. Let mistakes teach you but do not let them keep you stuck in the past.

Skipper Bruce was correct. Life experience is the best teacher, and there is no going back to undo the past. We realize we have made a mistake and we cannot turn back the hands of time to correct anything. Being human beings we all continue to make mistakes, and lots of them. The question now is this: what do we do with these mistakes? Do we sit and sulk and say "coulda, shoulda, woulda"? Do we get right back up and keep going forward as the crew on Skipper Bruce's schooner did in those days on the high seas? You know the answer.

It took Skipper Bruce many years to really forgive himself for that first day when I lost my first Atlantic salmon. When we went into town to a local convenience store, we realized what had gone wrong. Skipper Bruce had tied the wrong knot in the leader and it pulled through allowing the fish to break free with the hook in its mouth. For many years, Skipper Bruce mentioned this to people he knew, talking about the big salmon that got away on my very first day salmon fishing. He felt responsible for losing the fish. Now, I feel that it was better to lose that first one. It made for a better story.

Hooked on Real Life Learning

Someone once said that when the student is ready, the teacher usually appears. That statement best describes my relationship with Skipper Bruce. I was instantly hooked, not only with his unending kindness and love of life but by his unique ability to teach. He often commented while on our fishing expeditions "If we only knew the mind of a fish…" We will never know all the answers but we will learn more about ourselves in the "fishing" process. Here is one question to ask: How do we best maximize teaching and learning? Most of your real life teachings not only come from experience but from your own unique personal development or self-education. You are never too young or too old to strive for your life dream. Keep learning and keep going forward in the direction that you choose. Now is the time to get hooked – on YOU!

Chapter 1 Nuggets for Digestion:

~ Keep searching and you will find.
~ Dust off your childhood.
~ Spend time in Nature - therapy of the best kind.
~ "Work hard, play hard, but, be safe"… always.
~ Embrace change.
~ Learn from your mistakes.
~ Forgive yourself and move forward.
~ Find a solid teacher or mentor from whom to learn - even a silent mentor.
~ Get "hooked" on your own Personal Development- NOW!
~ Go "fishing" - but not for the fish.

2

It's MY Fault!

Almost all unhappiness in life comes from the tendency to blame someone else.
Brian Tracy

Responsibility, one of the main ingredients of life, is a concept that eludes many people. Some people understand it; however, many do not. I used to be one of those disgruntled individuals who did not know the meaning of responsibility. Several relatives often spoke about Skipper Bruce taking full responsibility for everything that happened to him. He not only "talked his talk" but he "walked his walk." They claimed he spoke highly of it as a main act of life. Years later, when I reflected on the life-long lessons that Skipper Bruce taught me, these teachings were evident.

I will always remember the time we were driving home from one of our fishing escapades. Coming into the town off the main highway, the speed limit rapidly changed. Skipper Bruce kept driving at the high speed while telling me a story. He was not paying attention to the speedometer. Sure enough, the beacons flashed on behind us. As Skipper Bruce was engrossed in the story, and had not seen the lights, the police officer made a short shriek with his siren to get our attention. We pulled over and waited for the officer to approach the car. Skipper Bruce took off his seatbelt and leaned sideways to get his wallet out of his back pocket.

When the officer came to the window he asked Skipper Bruce, "Did you know that you were speeding?"

Skipper Bruce replied "Yes, I was. I'm sorry. I was not paying attention. **It's my fault**."

The officer then asked him if he had been wearing his seatbelt. He said, "Yes, I just took it off, sir."

While the officer was writing the ticket, I asked Skipper Bruce, "What if the officer did not believe you regarding the seatbelt?"

He, then, assertively said, "The officer would have heard it!" Skipper Bruce went on to say "Speak out! Freedom of speech is our ultimate freedom. Many do not know what is right and they live in fear, but you have got to know your rights."

It was an interesting conversation and educational session we had that day. Skipper Bruce received his ticket and, with a great story to tell, we were on our way home chuckling about the incident. Many other people probably would not laugh. What's done is done and when you take responsibility, life goes on.

That story, about honesty and responsibility, became a classic family story and was told many times over the years. Two of my other relatives were also pulled over by the same police officer, in the same area, a few months apart. The lifelong lesson was learned. Many of my friends who have been pulled over by the police for speeding will often say that they were not going that fast. Speed radars, however, do not lie. At all times, the challenge for each of us is to be honest. I heard one parent say to his children, "Always be honest and tell the truth and you will never get in trouble." This is an excellent parenting expectation. Not only does it teach children to be honest, but also it allows children the ability to accept responsibility for their actions - a powerful way to teach solid morals and values. Open communication is also established and, as a result, daily problems and challenges can be better managed, and solved.

Skipper Bruce frequently advocated responsibility to many of my relatives. He meant that whatever the outcome, one was responsible for it. Why do some people not want to take responsibility, while others take complete responsibility? Life is the way it is and sometimes we cannot change it. The only thing we can change, as individuals, is our ability to respond in a positive productive way. In this sense, we have some control of the outcome. Many people have often heard the statement, "He does not take responsibility for anything." I have often heard it in the school system. Unfortunately, many youth do not learn responsibility at a young age. Maybe society has absolved individuals from taking responsibility. The lady who was burned when she spilled <u>her</u> hot coffee on <u>herself</u> after leaving the fast food restaurant is one example. She filed a lawsuit and won the case against the fast food corporation. Maybe the justice system has played a part. The trend is to absolve ourselves of responsibility; but as life is, it is always someone's fault.

Adjusting Your Approach

We are responsible for our results. Having finally accepted this idea, I realized life became more enjoyable. Every decision you have ever made, up to this moment has put this book in your hands. What a thought! The power in this statement comes in that six letter word, "change". If we are not getting the results we want it is best to change our course of action and change our thought processes. We cannot change much else and it has to start within. I learned this lesson while on the river.

Atlantic salmon often will not take my fly of choice. The reason is not clear. I do know, however, that I am responsible for the result. I, therefore, often change my fly to one smaller, bigger, a different color or different style. This often works like magic when fish are fussy and rise (Fly-fishing language calls a movement directed by a fish toward his/her fly a "rise.") to many flies but take none. Doing the same thing over expecting a different result just does not make sense. In changing our approach or changing our thought patterns, we accept full responsibility and we can change the outcome. We empower ourselves and this is what matters most.

Little changes can, amazingly, have a major result in the long-term. One change I did make in fly fishing was giving the salmon an extra second to take the fly in its mouth and close it. In my rookie years, I would lift the rod as soon as I observed the fish come near my fly. What was actually happening was the fish was rising, turning on the fly with its open mouth and I was pulling the fly away from the fish. Because of this, my overall results of fish hooked and retained, were low. I was raising a lot of fish but could not seem to solidly connect. Lots of "rises" but no results - it was time to change ... something.

A friend of my father told me, "Keep at it; lots of rises means you know how to attract the fish - a big step in this game." Once I learned that simple easy change of giving the fish one extra second or two to get the hook in its mouth, my success rates increased exponentially. One extra second! Wow! Once again, I was responsible for the outcome. What a feeling when you take responsibility! That extra second was very small, but many times that is all it takes.

A small change in philosophy or daily actions and the long term results can turn out to be extraordinary. Daily, we build new habits, and eventually get new and improved results. Daily walks, a daily vitamin, a daily positive comment are simple changes that have been known to help produce extraordinary future results. The small things in life often make a major difference.

Experts and Expertise

The self-proclaimed expert fly-fishermen I know can easily tell you what to do. If they know you have lost a fish during a battle, they can tell you what you should have done to prevent this from occurring. Yet, in a similar situation their results are seldom different. How easy it is to sit back and criticize someone else. There really are no experts. Experts defend their ideas that they have learned; however, in our world of constant change, knowledge based ideas are replaced frequently with newer, faster and better ones. The real "experts" I know are continuously learning new things both on the river and in life. They possess expertise but they are not experts.

Many self-proclaimed "expert" fly-fishermen will often make excuses for "the big one that got away." It is, however, **always** the fishermen's responsibility. Why put the fish in charge of the outcome? It is never the fish's fault. Once I accepted this, I knew I had the power to change. When the fish broke my leader, it was my fault. Sometimes the hook came out of the fish. Once again, it was my fault for not setting it properly.

Beware of "experts". One time, while I fished the Chute Pool on the Pinware River, I had the unique opportunity of experiencing two self-proclaimed experts tell me how to fish. I chuckled to myself about wisdom, fishing and expertise. No one hooked a fish that morning but, when they left and I had the pool to myself, things changed. I stepped back, fished my fly closer to shore and tried a few alternate techniques. As a result, I had more action than most anglers had for the rest of the week. Challenge what you see, hear and believe and then make your own decisions. Keeping an open mind in any situation will allow you to remain sharp on the life learning curve.

Thinking Responsibility

We are responsible for our thoughts and our feelings in life. As a counselor in the field of cognitive therapy, I learned that we act the way we feel and we feel the way we think. Thus everything starts from our thinking. Einstein asserts that: "Nothing happens until something moves". This can be applied to our thinking patterns. Thoughts really are things - electrical impulses with energy for transmission. Once we learn to control our thoughts, we can control almost every aspect of our lives. Habits, however, are easy to get into and hard break. Many of us have struggled trying to change defeating habits. We blame the government or the company or the school board or our spouses or whatever for our challenges and problems in life. I have done this as well. It serves no purpose other than preventing us from becoming better. Taking responsibility may be considered a conditioned habit and we need to be conditioned to take it.

Actions and words are crucial. Our self-talk is a vital component to everything in life. Think about what you are thinking about. When I go to the river or to a pond for fly-fishing, I try to keep my thoughts focused on the task at hand - being at peace with nature and anticipating a rise to the fly. I have often missed fish on the rise because I was focused on other things. Once I mastered this self-talk and realized that, while on the river, I must focus on the river and on nature, everything changed. We all know people who, while driving to work, are thinking about work. Oftentimes, they end up in a car accident because they are not focusing on the drive. Being responsible for the drive and getting to work safely must be a priority. At work is the best time to concentrate on work. We must not deceive ourselves in such situations of responsibility.

Some people believe that they can go to a weekend or evening seminar and totally transform everything in their lives. They are really only fooling themselves! It takes about one year on average to change a habit. It cannot really be eliminated; but, it must be replaced with another more productive habit. This takes time to solidify. We would like to believe that a one time transformational program will change us completely. A seminar can give you the ideas for change, but continuous personal development is required to reinforce the change process over time. There really is no other way.

Attitude is EVERYTHING!

Wayne Dyer states: "There is no way to happiness; happiness is the way." Skipper Bruce lived two decades with cancer eating away at his body, yet his attitude was remarkable. He certainly took responsibility and responded to his illness in a positive manner. His positive outlook on life and his unique ability to connect with people allowed him to remain on earth for an extended period of time. Cancer cannot be an easy battle for anyone.

Responding in a positive way is an important life concept. We all have our trials and tribulations, our ups and downs, our high points and low points in life. We know we are going to die. While on earth, make the most of it. It seems like those who respond in a positive way and have a solid attitude, as Skipper Bruce did, enjoy greater life success – with more productivity and more fun along the way.

When others achieve success, the pessimists in society often claim that they are "lucky". They fail to see the hours that went into the "lucky" accomplishment. Keeping the positive attitude and learning from setbacks is what separates the high achievers in life from the status quo. The "lucky" ones know how to respond with a positive attitude. Happiness and attitude are both choices. Not enough can be said about the importance of a positive, happy attitude. What are you choosing to think and feel today?

Fishy Response Moments

Just like in daily life situations, the angler will often get frustrated. In these moments, nothing seems to go right - the leader snaps, the hook cracks, the fish breaks free from the hook. Confidence in your ability is the most important aspect of fly-fishing and, probably, the most important aspect of any challenge in life.

One of my famous embarrassments happened on the Southeast River in Placentia, Newfoundland and Labrador. It was early season. The water was high and not many fish were showing. I knew the salmon were moving through the river fast because Mother Nature has a way of protecting her own. On this morning, around 9 AM, I went to a pool called the "One Mile". Fastened to my line was a battered Muddler Minnow fly, tied on a Mustad Accu-point hook. Ensuring I covered all the pockets of water, I proceeded down the river. During my first hour on the river, no fish were spotted or hooked. I knew they were moving through and I took a short break before fishing again.

The main One Mile pool was bursting with the fresh flow of an early summer rainfall. Birds chirped in the background and this helped ease my mind from the life's daily pressures. The surrounding scene was freshly painted green by Mother Nature. It was one of those "had to be there" moments. Not wasting too much time basking in the atmosphere, I stripped off some line and began my approach to the anticipated fish in the river. What a morning it was as I thought about Skipper Bruce and our trips together.

Having swept my fly across the main pool several times, I hauled off more line and flicked it to the far end of the pool and let it sweep naturally through the tail "vee" where the water emptied out. As the fly moved across the middle of the pool, my heart rate suddenly increased. A swirl underneath my fly caught my attention. Immediately, I flicked back the same cast, keeping the exact length of line out. This time, when the fly came across the pool, the swirl happened again. I lifted, expecting a big trout but, when my line went tight, the rod bent over and the reel started to sing. It was a fresh chunky Atlantic salmon. With one run down the river, jumping and flicking its whole body, it peeled off about 70 feet of fly line. The game was on!

Chasing the fish down the river, I tripped and fell. I kept the line tight, hoping the tension would beat the fish out faster. When the fish tired after four of five minutes, I, thinking it was a fat fresh hen or female salmon, dragged "her" close to shore. The fish was ready to be landed. With one scoop of my dip-net, I lifted the fish straight up. Unfortunately, it came right back out of the net, down near the water. Little did I know the mesh in the net was rotten! The fish plopped on the bank, flipping and flopping, trying to get back in the river.

I, of course, did the next worst thing. I tried to grab the fish by the tail, instead of, by the gills. With one flick, this stocky fish almost snapped my wrist! It certainly was GAME ON! The fly was still in the fish's mouth and the leader was still through the net attached to my rod which I had thrown on the bank. The leader was now wrapped around both of my wading boots. What a tangle!

I attempted to kick the fish further from shore. "Boom," the fish brought up solid against the muddy sod and ricocheted right back into the river. The leader was snapped instantly. With the river raging and, with my Muddler Minnow still hanging from its mouth, the fish flicked off on its side, as if to say, "Good bye. Thanks…but no thanks". I looked in disbelief as the fish slid nonchalantly sideways back into the main current. If someone had told me that story I probably would not have believed it. To this day, I still have a hard time telling it. After that loss, it took me about 45 minutes to calm down. So close, yet, so far away. The fisherman again was responsible.

After I lost that fish through the dip-net, I went into the local gas bar to chat with the owner. Because early in his career he was also an avid angler, the owner, an older gentleman, asked me about fishing. I told my story sprinkled with curses, in a humorous but serious way. He said, "No wonder you lost your salmon." His response to my attitude left me thinking. If my results were going to improve, my attitude had to improve. The words we speak are often a reflection of our feelings. The words we use every day have to be both positive and uplifting, not only for others, but most importantly for ourselves. Being positive and being happy attracts the same - on the river and in everyday life.

Responsible Negatives

Many people struggle with the idea of responsibility because they feel that it leads to blame. Blame is the negative way to see the result while empowerment is the positive way. Is blame a part of responsibility? It is if you believe it to be so. Responsibility means empowerment. Empowerment helps people accept error and allows them to take power to make necessary changes. Taking full responsibility means self-acceptance. The hardest picture you will ever see is a picture of yourself. We scrutinize ourselves more often than we would like to admit. We are blinded by the light that shines in the mirror and reflects the person that needs to change. At the same time, we often fail to see the shining star that does exist. It is there like the rainbow after a mid afternoon shower of rain, waiting to be observed and admired. We often must be somewhat self-centered as responsible human beings because if we do not take care of ourselves, who will?

Many people in our society struggle with being self-centered - the WIIFM (what's in it for me) syndrome. Have you been down that road? Admitting this is the hardest part. There is a need for self-centeredness, to take care of oneself first. At the same time, there is a need to help others. Self-centeredness is the solution to taking responsibility. Many people will place the blame on others when things do not go their way. These same people will want to take all the credit for the successes. Self-centered responsibility is a challenge. A different twist in thinking makes it possible to change our often selfish ways. In what ways have you been productively selfish and unproductively selfish? Maybe now is the time for you to change.

Choice and Chance

We were all born into this world as innocent children. Some parents have not been loving and supportive. We have all been through some of that "stuff." What happens to us tends to happen to everybody in some way, shape or form. Some people have cancer, some people have diabetes, some people suffer addictions or eating disorders, and some people have been diagnosed learning disabled and do not perform well academically in structured school settings. My father would call it our individual "crosses to the bear". As adults, it is time to take complete responsibility for our lives. That is the only answer. In taking complete responsibility, we create, and have control, over the outcome. If we do not create the outcome, someone else will. What a scary idea! Do not take such a chance.

Life may be considered a game of choice, not a game of chance. We choose, most importantly, our ability to respond. If we choose a positive response and accept that we have made a mistake, life will often work out well. I remember fishing the Branch River with a friend of mine. Traveling over the rough ground on the all-terrain vehicles was quite an adventure. It took us almost as much time on the all-terrain vehicles as it would have if we had to walk.

When we arrived at our fishing destination and were unloading our fishing supplies, I opened my plastic rod case and saw that both my fly rods were cracked off. How disappointing! Even though they were on my buddy's bike, I was responsible. I did not know that I should have placed the rod case lengthwise, going with the bike, instead of across the back on the rack. The rod case buckled when we went down in one of the bog holes. On the way out of the hole, the case snapped back into place and my rods were instantly shattered. I managed to tape the bottom end of one rod to the top piece of the other rod. This was not a perfect combination. The top piece of the second rod was split; however, it was good enough to fly fish that day.

On this day of learning and adventure, the river was low; yet, I did have some action. In a little pocket of water near the lower falls, I raised a dandy salmon three or four times. Lifting the rod and trying to keep it together with both hands, I was too slow. The fly swept into the corner of the salmon's mouth. I missed the fish three or four times and she did not return. Leaving that day, I accepted complete responsibility. I had cracked both rods and, as a result, my mother did not get a fresh salmon for supper. No one did it to me. I was completely responsible.

If it is to be it is up to me!

These 10 two-letter words exemplify a simple yet powerful concept in responsibility. In making mistakes, we learn ways not to repeat the past. One of my favorite childhood stories was, and still is, *The Little Engine That Could*. "I think I can, I think I can, I think I can" are words that my mother repeated over and over to me. That powerful childhood phrase was further solidified in my conscience by Skipper Bruce. Not only his words, but also his positive attitude allowed me to believe that I could do anything I put my mind to, no matter what I had done in the past. It has allowed me to create my reality and my world and it will do the same for you. As adults, we must realize that if we do not complete a task, no one will do it for us. We must choose to be as educated as possible regarding life responsibility. Further, we must choose to go ahead and make things happen because, as responsible adults know, this is the only way for achievement to occur.

Some anglers will not move the net when helping a fellow angler "dip" or retrieve a fish once it is near the shore to be landed. They will hold the net in an open area and let the angler bring the fish to the net. In this way, the "dippers" are not responsible if the hook pops out, if the leader breaks, or if the net snaps the line and the fish is lost. In such cases, as it should be, the major responsibility is placed on the angler. In your life the major responsibility is on you.

Many beginning young salmon anglers have their friends or family hook a salmon and let them play it out to either tag or release it. This used to be illegal and I have done it a couple of times in the past to help out a fellow angler. This legality in salmon fishing is one that helps promote responsibility. If the angler cannot hook and catch the salmon, then they should not have the privilege to retain it. Teaching someone the proper procedure to hook and capture an Atlantic salmon, on their own, is what matters most. They are responsible for the result. We are not out to 'get fish' but to get better at fishing, and at life.

Chapter 2 Nuggets for Digestion:

~ It is always someone's fault; take responsibility.
~ Know your rights as a free thinking citizen.
~ Speak out and practice your freedom of speech.
~ We cannot undo the past; be responsible and move forward.
~ Be honest; the truth does make us free from past junk.
~ Practice open communication with the people in your life.
~ Be careful of "experts".
~ You are only an expert on one person: YOU!
~ It takes one year on average to change a habit.
~ Focus on the task at hand; pay attention.
~ Speak only positive words.
~ Become positively self-centered.
~ Life is a game of choice; choose wisely.
~ If it is to be, it is up to YOU!

3

On The Rocks

We learn best from life's experiences, especially our mistakes.
Skipper Michael Joseph Bruce

Even though life experience is the best teacher, it is often a harsh teacher. Unlike formal schooling, the University of Life usually gives you the test first and the lesson afterwards. Skipper Bruce had a limited formal education; yet, he was one of the most intelligent human beings I have ever known. He could carry on a conversation with the most advanced scholar. His lessons were often very simple and his teaching methods reflected that simplicity. In order for me, as a young boy, to grasp his ideas and values, Skipper Bruce used simple teaching methods tinged with much laughter and fun. Simplicity also works well with adult learners. Some would argue that many adults are stuck in childhood and have not grown up. This may be true, but keeping your childhood curiosity will keep you learning for life.

Bona Fide Skippers

Many of the things we learn in university or college will never be applied to real life. Maybe they are not meant to be. These formal schooling concepts do help us think through problems. Knowledge for knowledge sake is fine, but sharing knowledge for personal development sake is where Skipper Bruce excelled.

Many of our self-made millionaires have a grade 12 education level or less. What an interesting fact! Many of these people went through the "school of hard knocks" to become financially successful. Life experience often teaches us how to turn our lives around for the better. Have you ever been through the "school of hard knocks" and survived? Reflecting on our past mistakes and sharing our insight with others can maximize our learning experience.

Skipper Bruce, having learned honesty at an early age from his father, now passed his message on to me. While his father and the crew gathered rest, Skipper Bruce was placed in charge of the schooner. As he was also tired on this shift, he dozed off a few times. His father checked on him from time to time and found him asleep. When he denied this to his father, Skipper Bruce learned one of his greatest lessons - the lesson of honesty.

His father took him aside and said, "Mike, you were asleep and, as skipper, you have command of the ship and our crew. Our lives are in your hands and you must stay awake." It was not only the words that conveyed the meaning this day, but also the emotional vigor and sincerity that his father used to deliver his message. This day on the high seas, when Skipper Bruce lied to his father, was the last time that he ever remembered telling a lie. Honesty is not only the best policy; but it is also the foundational rule of life. When we fail to tell the truth, we are only being dishonest with ourselves. His father often told him, "Mike, you'll be skipper someday". When the time was right, he did become Skipper. When Skipper Bruce told me this story, tears of joy came to his eyes as he relived the experience with his father about real life leadership and walking a new road. There are no shades of honesty; we are either honest or not. Real leaders are honest

Rocky Roads

Benjamin Disraeli once stated: "There is no education like adversity." My first experience with fly fishing for large (greater than 10 pounds) Atlantic salmon was on the Pinware River, Labrador, Canada, June 2000. At that time, I was "stuck" in life. I had finished university and was unsure what to do next. What a trip it was! I was instantly hooked on the beauty of the scenery, the people and the BIG fish that thrived there. It was a great way to start a rocky road adventure off the island of Newfoundland into unknown territory, Ontario, Canada, where I later moved.

Running from my problems and, more importantly, from myself, I fought to make sense of life in Ontario. For several years, I battled depression. After many painful tears, I was learning how to manage myself. Our problems follow us, wherever we go. At times, the challenges often magnify until they are solved. In 2004, I returned to Newfoundland to complete my Masters Degree and found a job as school counselor in Labrador. It was here that I learned my valuable lesson in self-honesty and character. We all need to learn this lesson.

The books and documentaries are endless regarding the setbacks and tough times that people experience to strengthen their characters and keep them surviving. We know the stories of Oprah Winfrey, Jim Carrey and Stephen King. We also know the stories of those close to home. Our own stories fall into this category. A good friend of mine lost his formal wear business in a devastating fire in 2003. After the smoke cleared, he was over $950,000 in debt! Did he cry? Yes. Did he want to quit? Yes. Did he experience a rough road? Yes. Five years later, after much hard work, he is back on his feet, close to being debt free and he still provides the best customer service in the industry. We can conclude that he had one of those life-changing moments. Because he used the experience to fix what needed to be fixed, both personally and professionally, his choice brought him to a better place. Have you ever had such a life changing experience?

The Day

June 25, 2005 at Guy's Point on the Pinware River, Labrador, where I had made my first cast for Atlantic salmon, was the day that changed me forever. Six years prior, I landed my first 12 pound Atlantic salmon. Isn't it funny how things come full circle in life? Jim Rohn, my silent mentor, who has been hailed as the World's Leading Business Philosopher, calls it "The day that turns your life around."

The river was crowded that evening. One of my favorite "hot spots", Guy's Point, above the bridge on the left-hand side looking up the river, however, was vacant. I parked my car and quickly hiked by the Pinware River Lodge on the trail to the pool. Progressing down to Guy's Point, I could see that I was alone. Many anglers were fishing on the other side of the river and some stood on the bridge watching the evening's action. Because the water level was low for this time of the year, few fish were being hooked. When the fish are "running" in peak season, the Pinware River Bridge, about 100 feet above the river, makes for a great view of the scenery and action.

I hustled down to the pool. Placing my packsack down at the head of the pool, I quickly put together my fly-fishing rod - a 10 foot Sage "battle-stick" that cost me a small fortune. Something did not feel right. I felt somewhat sick. Unsure of what was happening and maybe wanting to fish before anyone else showed up, I rushed to present my fly in the low water condition of the river. After five or six casts, I hooked a nice grilse, or a small salmon, on a "white wing blue charm" fly. Playing him out, as he wanted to go down the river into the next pool, I struggled. Even though he was tired, the fish did not want to come to shore. Finally, it came near enough to be handled. Beaten out from exhaustion, the fish went bottom up. I picked the fresh salmon up by the gills and threw it in the nearby rocks. As I felt the urge for candy, I immediately went back to my pack sack about 50 feet away. Having type-one insulin dependent juvenile diabetes (4 needles per day) for over 24 years, my blood sugar was feeling dangerously low. Before exercising, I had given my needle, yet I had not eaten what I should have. Being in a rush can have deadly results.

Not finding any candy, I remember heading back down towards my fish. Having a few more casts and fishing along the way, I realized the tag was not in the fish as it was supposed to be. Conservation measures in Newfoundland and Labrador allow for only a certain number of Atlantic salmon that must be tagged with proper tags immediately after retention. My mind was aloof at this point and my blood sugar felt treacherously low.

As I took another step down the river, in the direction of my catch, I saw two wardens running towards me. Positioning my rod safely on a rock, I walked towards them and introduced myself. They did not respond. One of the wardens asked me for my license. As I went to tag my fish, he demanded, "Don't touch that fish." I sat on a rock and complied with what he had said, conserving energy, wondering where my candies were. I knew, then, I had made a mistake. The fish was not tagged.

Well, I did then what I had been conditioned to do in life and what many people are conditioned to do. I lied to them, saying how I went back to my pack sack to get my knife because I wanted to clean the fish before tagging it. Many of us are embarrassed to admit imperfections, especially about our health. Who can explain why we sometimes do not tell the truth up front? It happens for many of us at one point or another. Maybe now I understand what the word "immediately" means - immediately doing what is right and protecting my health, the bigger picture in the story.

One of the wardens tried to play "Matlock" and solve the case before I was charged. At this point, I said nothing and sat on the rock wondering where the sugar was. The conservation officers, informing me that I would be charged, left. When the wardens departed with my fish, tag, and fly-rod, I slowly proceeded up the river and sat on a nearby cliff overlooking a still pool in the river. I checked my blood sugar and it was 2.2 mmol/dl (normal is 5.0). The sugar level in my blood was seriously low. Sitting down once again, I discovered the candy were in my vest all along. I ate them all as quickly as I could. Twenty-two candies later and here I was, waiting for my sugar level to increase so I could think straight. A life changing thought occurred to me.

Looking out at the pool, with the sun trying to break the clouds as it set in the west, I could see a reflection of my greatest problem and my only solution ... ME! I proceeded to have a stern discussion with myself, about this incident, about life, about honesty, about my health and about things that really matter, to me.

After 25-30 minutes, I retested my blood sugar and it was 7.4 mmol/dl. It was now normal according to the sugar meter. Walking back to my car, I was disappointed, in me. I drove to my apartment in the community where I worked and I wrote in my journal what had just happened. I am thankful, today, that the wardens did arrive. They probably saved my life. I am also thankful that the river was low. With high water, I would probably have fallen in. Life's toughest lessons always bring out the best in us. That day my life was "on the rocks". That day my life changed. Everyone experiences daily disappointments and frustrations. This is part of life. Humans make mistakes. The challenge to become better contributing members of society is the reason we exist. It is as if our creator has given us our talents to see what we can and will do with them.

Recently, I have concluded that fly fishing is one of my means to peace of mind and solitude. Skipper Bruce had taught me the ways of the woods and the waters for a reason. Now, I could share these lessons with others. Making mistakes is easy. Learning from them is the hard part. Some people continue to make the same mistakes over and over again without learning. We have all experienced this at some point in life. Our greatest setbacks are usually our greatest learning experiences. Have you experienced "the day that will turn your life around" yet?

Learning By Doing

Skipper Bruce pointed out that one of the best ways of learning is learning from our mistakes. Mistakes help teach responsibility. A lesson is repeated until learned. In my second year of salmon fishing, I remember going to a pool below "the cliff" on the Southeast River in Placentia, Newfoundland. The water was high and I was not crafty at casting the fly in the river. As I worked my way down the river, my wet fly sailed across the stream, letting the current do all the work. As the fly neared the end of its sweep, a fresh, frisky Atlantic salmon came right out of the water and nailed my offering, hooking itself on impact. My line went tight and, with both hands on the rod and reel, I held the fish. Without delay, it went to the bottom of the pool where the water was rushing in. I could feel the fish move back and forth with its head against the rocks trying to scrape the hook out of its mouth.

Finally, I turned my rod sideways and, with one pull, I managed to get the fish to move. It made a springing leap about ten feet in the air and made its way down the river with a vengeance. Lacking experience in playing out fish and letting them run until tired, I did what just about every salmon angler does at one point or another in his or her fishing career. With my hands on the line, while squeezing the handle, I barred the fish tight. I did not let the reel do its work. Snapping the line with one echoing "*POP*", the fish broke free. Another lesson was learned on the steep learning curve of a beginning angler: do not hold anything too tight or it may break free. We all need to let things go. Only then can we best learn what the experience has to teach us.

Stumbling Forward

Steppingstones can lead to life success and a bright future. Viewed another way, stepping stones can be seen as stumbling rocks. Some people see the stones as something to fall over; while others see them as something to stand on and jump over. Perception, like beauty, is in the eye of the beholder. In cognitive therapy, we follow the law of perception: we all see things differently. It would have been so easy for me to give up fly fishing during those early five years. I know now that it was never about the fish but about the person I was becoming - a better fisherman, and human being.

The steppingstones, that we fall over and eventually learn to climb over, help shape our abilities not only to "attract fish", but also to get back up quickly. We cannot really change the past. We can, however, certainly learn from it. We get to stand on the stones that often trip us up and, eventually, when the time is right, we learn to avoid those rocks altogether.

Slippery Caution

Certain rivers have very slippery rocks. Before getting my felt bottom waders, I would often fall and stumble. When we fall down, it hurts. The rocks can be viewed as negative people in life who try to hold us back or trip us up along the way. We must rise above these rocks to where the water is fast, the pace is high, and the learning is immense. In a river, the water on top of the current is often the fastest and brightest; while the undercurrent is often sluggish and contains the most filth.

The challenge for you is to become like the water on top, rising above and avoiding the negativity and people in life who try to bring you down. Gossip mongrels are burdened and unable to move. Skipper Bruce often warned me to "Be careful of 'slippery' people." Whether we realize it or not, they can do a lot of damage. What is most challenging is sending these people some of your love energy. This is what they are searching for in their own internal life battles. The gossipers and disgruntled ones often lack self-love. They lack the sense of self-worth. As difficult as this may seem, it is best to send them, via warm thoughts, some of our love. It will only make us better in the long term.

Skipper Bruce explained the danger in these "slippery" people. They will do anything and everything to better themselves in places of power, employment, and finances - at the expense of others. How right he was, and is, being a "big fish in a small pond." It is time for you to be like the water on top of the stream: fresh, clear and free from filth. Further, the challenge is to be like Skipper Bruce: a BIG and wise fish, which does not get fooled. Large fish grow that way for a reason – they do not get caught. One self-proclaimed expert angler told me one time that "There are no 20 pound salmon in this river!" I knew they existed in this river after having hooked one and seeing another released. Just because the expert could not fool and hook one of these big fish did not mean that they did not exist.

Serious Reflective Study

In avoiding the negativity in life and striving to maximize our productivity, serious life study is required. We must study life, study people and study the environment around us. Yes, we are all students in the University of Life, going somewhere. The lesson I learned happened when trying to capture "sulky" salmon. Sulky salmon often rise to the surface for many flies, but will not take a single one. Arthur Wood, one of the greatest Atlantic salmon anglers of all time, said that any fish rising comes to the fly because it means business. Even though the fly is often not taken, the intent was there and it is the responsibility of the angler to capture the fish using his or her skills and expertise. I undertook serious study, reading every book I could on fly fishing, watching videos, and talking to the veteran retired anglers. I figured that these veteran anglers often knew something that many do not. I was right. Some of the tips, shared over the years, have landed me salmon. Other people had previously fished these waters to no avail.

The size of the fly is one such tip. Many people will use large flies when smaller versions are sometimes the best choice. In the eyes of the fish, small is more natural looking. Bigger is not always better. In order to thrive in different river situations, serious study of fishing helps maximize learning. The same lesson can be applied to your business, health, relationships and personal success. Do you constantly study and apply what you learn?

The basic ideas gathered from people, books and life experience help us in whatever path we choose. You cannot learn everything overnight. Why pave a new road when one has already been created? It is wise to study the mistakes of others and, of course, to study the successes of others. Seven years of university did not teach me this. I learned it when I went to work on myself, studying those who had been in the school of "hard knocks." Reflecting on you and on others, who have made life mistakes, is a small step in the direction forward. Your future is determined by your actions. Hopefully, you have come to the same fork in the road. When it is time to tear up your old life plan and prepare a new one, remember that the little things count.

Sometimes the damage of the small fly is more of a threat to a naturist than the thought of a black bear attack. Very rarely will a black bear attack a fisherman on the river. This is not to say it is not impossible, but unlikely. In particular, preparation, in such cases, tells us to avoid going near momma bear with her cubs. If a bear does attack, it is best to have your fly rod held high or another object held high to appear superior to the black bear. More often than not the little black flies and mosquitoes have the potential, as the saying goes, to "eat you alive". They break concentration and interfere with fishing presentation. Oftentimes, I will inhale the pests because they are so thick and abundant in Mother Nature.

Labrador is a prime example where the flies have the potential to wreak havoc on any fishing trip. Without a strong wind and some good fly oil, combined with onion or garlic breath, one does not have a chance for peace and solitude with nature. I remember someone once telling me that "grubby" anglers rarely get bitten by the flies. Someone well-groomed gets the most damage. I guess this is why some of my buddies, when they go on a fishing trip, refuse to shower for four to five days. In the end, they do not smell like freshly cut roses, but they are content to have all their blood and very few fly bites. Whether we realize it or not, the little things in life do have the greatest impact on us.

We all need challenges to help us grow. Sometimes like the salmon in the flowing river, we can take the path of least resistance. It is not wise to do this all the time. We need challenges, we need goals, and we need dreams. There is no better time than NOW for making the necessary adjustments. If your life has been "on the rocks" you do not have to stay there…just make a choice to find your way. Life experience is your toughest, but, best teacher.

Chapter 3 Nuggets for Digestion:

~ We learn best from life experience.
~ Simplicity is an excellent learning approach.
~ Keep your childhood curiosity.
~ Teach your life lessons to others to help them learn.
~ Honesty is still the foundational life policy.
~ Choose to get "unstuck".
~ Never run from your problems; they always follow and increase until solved.
~ The beginning of message is "mess".
~ Take advantage of the "day that turns your life around."
~ Do not rush the important things in life.
~ We are often our greatest problems, but also our ONLY solutions.
~ A lesson is repeated until fully mastered.
~ Do not hold anything too tight or it may break free.
~ Be careful of slippery rocks…and people.
~ The little things in life are often the most important.
~ If your life has been "on the rocks" now is the time to decide to change it!
~ "You'll be skipper someday" if you believe it!

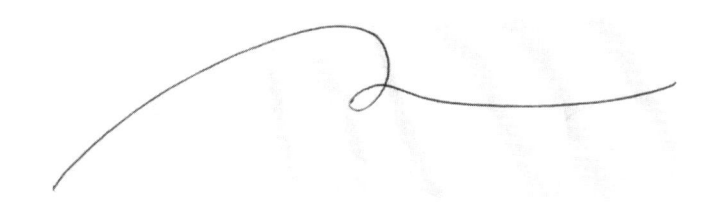

4

The Way to a Man's Heart…

*The greatest love of all, is easy to achieve;
Learning to love yourself, it is the greatest love of all.*
Whitney Houston (words and music by Michael Masser and Linda Creed)

When I left university my heart was cold and hard. I was bitter and angry at the world, at the government, at my parents and at life. My heart needed to be softened. My passion, fly-fishing, gave me meaning and happiness. I thought that it was all I had. From fly-fishing, I discovered peace and solitude. To know ourselves, we need to go inside and discover what we are all about - a difficult process to undertake. Often we do not like what we see. While trying to cope inwardly, we fight outwardly with our demons. Looking in the mirror for answers can be a difficult task.

Many of us never learn to love and appreciate ourselves for who we are. Society often dictates that, to be important, we must have material wealth. Dr Wayne Dyer, in his book *The Power of Intention* calls this our "ego." Our ego gets in the way of self-discovery. We often think that to be somebody, we must possess things and acquire social status. Why, then, do many people who have very little, love themselves so much? Why do they stay happy? From their inner nature, they have discovered self-love. Helping someone understand their inner nature is what I was searching for, and I finally found it. In searching, I did find answers to my problems and challenges. When you search, you will find answers. Often you will find much more.

Doing Better, Yet the Same

While it is true that many people are doing better than others, the fact is that no one IS any better than anyone else. We breathe the same air and live on the same planet. Because false beliefs and attitudes are everywhere, it takes time to see this. Your "do" is not your "who." The real value is in the doer, not the deed. In this regard, Skipper Bruce was an exceptional man. He could and would strike up a conversation with anyone to learn something new. Some flaunt the false belief that they are superior human beings. In reality, we are more alike than different. As a species, we are the same. Do not be fooled by those who try to make you believe otherwise. Being the same, we each share the same rooted feelings that must be acknowledged for growth to occur.

A t-shirt, I once wore, revealed the phrase: "The way to a man's heart is through his fly". What stares and smirks I received when wearing it. Some may have different meanings for this phrase. I, however, know the real meaning. Before I could love another I first had to love myself. Before I could enjoy another person I first had to learn to enjoy myself. The common denominator in all of this is personal development, becoming better from the inside first.

Personal development is a lifelong process. No matter what field or career you choose to pursue, as a start, you need to love YOU. This idea came to me not long into my new quest for a better life. Self-healing meant digging to the root of the problem. First, I had to forgive myself and move onward. If we are to move onward, we must let go of the past. This is part of the balance that our bodies and minds continually seek. When it is not achieved, we cannot move onward.

Life is a delicate balance. Some people are doing so financially well in their careers that it has overtaken them and their families have abandoned them. Would we call this a successful balance? No. Our greatest balancing act involves relationships. Friends and family, colleagues, spouses - all make up this relationship mix. How do we create great relationships? Seek the answers from those who have succeeded. The first piece of the puzzle involves your greatest friend and best enemy at times, the one staring at you in the mirror, talking to you 24 hours each and every day - YOU!

Self-Love - The Missing Piece of Your Puzzle

We all must start somewhere. Why not start with your heart and that mysterious feeling called love? Learn to love and appreciate yourself first and foremost. Some "experts" claim that love is the greatest value and feeling in existence. A sad reality of life is that many of us never really understand love. When I started to really love me, it was amazing. This book would never have been completed, had I not filled my self-love tank and increased my feelings of self-worth. Looking in the mirror, I started to appreciate me for who I am, with my unique set of talents and challenges. Fly-fishing was the starting point of self-discovery. Beginning all those years ago with Skipper Bruce, the way to my heart and soul was found on the Salmon River. What passion do you love that will help you discover who you really are? Mother Nature offers us answers if we visit her with an open mind. Take the time to reflect and discover who you are.

We cannot give away that which we do not have. Once the self-love tank is full, it is easy to forgive, to move forward, and to help other people. Before attempting to help anybody else, personally or professionally, top up your own tank. It makes sense logically and emotionally. When I feel good about me, I am better able to help others. Taking care of the person in the mirror is the first rule of order. What do you see when you look in the mirror? Can you look in the mirror and say "I love you"? Many people cannot. Before we can do anything for another human being, though, we must be responsible for our own lives. We must first love ourselves.

For many of us, the battle continues daily. Those of us who have gone through it know the feeling that comes when we learn to touch our inner souls and really appreciate ourselves for who we are. Maybe that is the reason I seemed addicted to fly-fishing at one point. It felt, at times, like this was all I had. In order to seek approval from my parents and friends, I wanted to become competent at the sport. In reality, I did not need to seek approval from anyone else. I needed only to seek approval from me. A small change in thinking allowed me to feel and act this new way. Self-love begins with self-esteem.

Self-Esteem Building

Our self-esteem is that unique feeling that we are worthy of life and happiness. How do we build up our self-esteem when we have been haunted by the past? Dysfunctional families are everywhere. Growing up in homes where parents are not in harmony is a major determinant of low self-esteem. Let the past teach you what not to do. Do not go back and relive it. Let the past teach you, but, do not let it rule you. Let the past be your teacher, not your master - easy to say, yet often hard to do. I know. Having worked with several individuals who have "fallen through the cracks" and having helped them overcome some fears I, now, believe there is an answer. Build your self esteem by your own efforts. Start small with the daily **positive** things you do well. You may need to start with saying "I like you" (in the mirror) and fake it until you make it.

Always take your life into your own hands and do not rely on others to add anything to it. With diligence and determination, work on your own personal development. Having come through rough and rugged life experiences, many have succeeded. You must start somewhere. Even though no book can really fix us, it is often the idea within the book that leads to another idea, another book, or another personal experience that helps start the self-development process. Self-esteem comes from self.

Our lack of self-esteem can be traced to our lack of belief in self. The field of sport psychology teaches people that performance **always** follows belief in self. We do not perform and, then, believe; we believe and, then, perform. Lacking belief in your natural abilities is not a formula for success, happiness and self-love. Social scientists have told us that each human being has a unique set of inborn talents. Each person is a piece of the whole community and, if given the opportunity to develop his or her talents, society would benefit greatly. Going to work on your own unique abilities is the answer to a better future. Filling up your love and esteem tank can only aid in this process. Our associations with colleagues, friends, and family have enormous impact on our self-esteem because we have been conditioned to let them affect us in a variety of ways. It is easy to see which associations are destructive and which ones are constructive. The answer is simple: only associate long term with constructive people, as it will benefit you and them.

Go to a coffee shop for a mid-morning break. We often hear people complain about their jobs and their lives. They are actually complaining about themselves. Maybe they have not discovered their unique talents and they lack belief in their abilities. In doing so, their self-esteem stays low and they cannot grow. I was one of these people…lost. Once I changed me, my self-esteem grew. Part of this process involved weeding my garden of the destructive poison from people who did not belong there. It can happen to all of us when we are not careful. How have your closest associations been influencing you? Is it time to make changes for a better future?

Keep your mental filter on high, knowing that many negative forces are trying to hold you back in your journey forward. That is the way life operates and we can be certain this will not change! People falsely believe that competition, with each other, benefits them. It seems sometimes that life is "survival of the fittest" raised one level on the hierarchy, so people will not eat each other in competition. Self-esteem, the foundational block of self-love and all of life happiness, must be measured inwardly because we are only better than we used to be. We are not better than anyone else. Making those changes in thinking and acting is how your better future starts. When you make those little changes in getting rid of negative associations for the sake of your feelings of self-esteem, your life will change for the better. Things only change when you do.

Inevitable Change

From this lifelong learning journey, change has to be embraced. I read one time that, after three years, the majority of the cells in the human body have been replaced by new cells. We are a work in progress. Change is reality...and inevitable. In one meeting I attended, a lady was all 'gung ho' about going to a Third World country to help the citizens. She was obsessed with changing the world. In her next three breaths, I experienced her gossiping about her colleagues! Change must initially start from the inside or we act hypocritically. Wanting to save the starving citizens in the world is a worthy ideal, but change, like charity, begins at home. I am sure you have witnessed such experiences.

Change is one constant about which we can be certain. On the Salmon River, there are no two exact moments in time. Every second the river changes. Biochemical processes, such as riverbanks washing in, rocks being over-turned, and acid levels fluctuating, happen to further change the environment. Life change, too, is constant. Through technological advancements, opportunities for unlimited possibilities have opened around the globe. The numbers of people in jets flying everywhere, cities being further developed and new buildings being constructed is hard to comprehend…but it is happening. We must embrace this change.

Thinking and Getting Better

Thoughts become things. This idea in the personal development journey can change your life. In cognitive therapy, we help people control and manage situational depressions just by challenging and, often, disputing the unrealistic thoughts that come to mind. Often medication is needed when someone is affected by metabolic depression (family genetics causing predisposition to the illness).

There has been some serious debate between psychologists and psychiatrists about the best way to approach mood disorders such as depression. Some psychologists believe that everything can be controlled by your thinking; while some psychiatrists believe totally in the medical model. Because you own your body, the best approach is for the individual to find what works best.

When someone is affected by a severe mental illness, before any therapy can work effectively it often takes a medical doctor's precision. Following this adjustment, the client is able to use the self-help approach required for living a balanced life. In this instance, a combination of medication and talk-therapy works effectively. What may work for some clients will not work for all clients. Once again the key is to self-discover what works best for you regarding a medical illness and regarding your life.

The human body, like life, always seeks homeostasis - a delicate operating balance. Once out of balance, the body, and the mind, tries to return to its original state. Changing behaviors, such as thinking patterns, is often difficult. The body is used to the old system and does not like the new approach. We must condition the new and let go of the old in order to become better.

There is a difference, however, between feeling better and getting better. With a change in thoughts, feeling better can happen instantly. Further a slight change in actions will also aid this process. Not consuming alcohol because it is a depressant is one such behavior recommended for those who suffer with depression. It makes sense if one wishes to feel better. Getting better, on the other hand, takes time. When we attempt to eliminate a bad habit or change some area of life that needs adjusting, many of us learn this. Complete habit change is not going to take place overnight.

Something to Ponder

Simple arithmetic reveals that we have 24 hours in a day. There are 168 hours in one week. Supposing we go on a two-day, weekend self-improvement program for 5 hours per day. The time now is 10 hours of self-development. If you are 30 years of age, it means you have over 262,000 hours of past conditioning. At 40 years of age you now have almost 350,000 hours of past conditioning. Ten hours is not going to eliminate the several hundred thousand hours of past learning no matter what a life coach or transformational specialist will want you to believe. The 10 hours can be a powerful start in the right direction but the positive momentum and self discipline must continue for lasting life change to transpire and remain.

Instant gratification does not work. Because new patterns must be formed and conditioned, changing a habit takes a minimum of about six months to one year. Non productive habits, feelings, thoughts, and ideas must be replaced with healthier ones; they cannot just be eliminated. When the earth is removed and a hole is created near the sea, water will fill up that hole. Fill the holes in your life with new healthier habits. If past experiences protrude and affect our everyday living, we must learn to heal ourselves by letting go of the thoughts that bind us. Then with new actions, such as a new exercise program or healthier eating, the improved habits will materialize.

Healing from the Inside

Developing our emotions is another aspect of personal development. Healing ourselves can be difficult because we must learn to educate our emotions. Men, in particular, often find this difficult. The tough and rugged image of the dominant male is a fallacy. The stronger a man exhibits the "real male tough self-image", the more he needs to get at his heart, build up his self-esteem, and heal for the better. Many men have never been instructed to educate their emotions. How do we do this? Experience from successful people teaches us to feel our feelings, cry when necessary and practice being human at every opportunity. Many of us, while growing up, were conditioned to suppress everything. In doing so, we did not learn how to feel. "Real men" are thought, and taught, to be rugged and tough. For them, starting to feel emotions can be frightening. In response, they often shut down or act out in ways that are hurtful.

Learning to love yourself primarily for who you are is the first step in the right direction. Because it is a learned behavior, it can be learned at any age! Moreover, negative behaviors can also be unlearned in the process. May the way to your heart be found in a passion, talent, hobby or activity that you can put to work in order to attain all of the important treasures valuable to you. Yes, the time is NOW to start loving you for who you really are. And in the words of Skipper Bruce after hearing about a successful catch or achievement, "Well done yourself!"

Chapter 4 Nuggets for Digestion:

~ Learn to love the person in the mirror first and foremost - YOU!
~ Soften your heart.
~ Search and you will find answers.
~ You are only better than you used to be; you are not better than anyone else.
~ YOU are the value, not the accomplishments or material stuff.
~ We are more alike than different as humans.
~ Forgive others and forgive yourself.
~ Life seeks balance so you must also seek balance.
~ You cannot give away that which you do not possess.
~ You only need to seek approval from YOU!
~ Do not rely on other people to add to your life.
~ Build up your own self esteem, one step at a time.
~ Belief always precedes performance.
~ People who complain are only complaining about themselves.
~ Be careful of your associations with other people.
~ Getting better and feeling better are two different phenomena.
~ Educate your emotions; feel your feelings; never suppress anything.
~ May the way to your heart be found through your passion.

5

Yes Man, Yes Maam!

As so often happens when people are seduced by promises of power, the price is servitude and impotence. Power is nothing if it is not the power to choose.
Joseph Weizenbaum

We have to associate with other people. What a boring life it would be if we lived all alone. At one time or another, many of us have felt alone. The challenge in life is to deal effectively with others once our own self-tanks have been filled. What a challenge this can be! It sometimes seems that life would be great if we did not have to deal with other people. Further, we may feel trapped by others who try to control us. What are the first three letters of the word, "manipulation"? Maybe you have felt one time or another, like a puppet with someone pulling your strings. Frustrating, isn't it? If we seek them out, there are answers to such situations.

Skipper Bruce stood his ground with fellow human beings and construction managers. He said, "No one is better than you or me, so speak out". How right he was. Human nature is mysterious at times. Why do some people want to control other people? When one seeks to have power over another, it usually means one lacks self-control. Maybe some are seeking to fill an internal void with external measures. Whatever the case may be, we must be careful with power and with the people who misuse it. Skipper Bruce often quoted Lord Acton's phrase, "Power corrupts; absolute power corrupts absolutely". Too much power can be dangerous. Be cautious in your journey.

Multiplying Simple Logic

Power only multiplies when it is shared and distributed within a team. If we take a large bag of lawn fertilizer and dump it in one pile on the grass, what happens? The grass is going to burn up with acidity. Too much concentration in one area causes destruction. The same holds true for power. For best results, it must be shared. What happens when the fertilizer is spread throughout the lawn? The grass grows green and bright, flourishing the soil with nature's beauty.

New age students and employees want to work as part of a team. Concentrated power in an institution often creates unhappiness and an unnecessary hierarchy of ideals. We see it daily and question it. Those who do not see it either do not want to or are afraid of losing power. Power is hard to let go. Shared power is one possible way to avoid corruption. Need we look any further than Hitler in Nazi Germany? We must learn from lessons of the past. Jim Rohn is correct: "Tyranny knows no restraint of appetite."

Like power, money only multiplies when it is shared with others. Those holding stocks in a business are called "shareholders." Investing money really means putting money into an account to be shared by others and, in turn, gaining interest on the investment. When we share ideas, the same happens. If something works well for you, pass it on to help another. We never know the power we have in sharing simple ideas and the long term effect these ideas may have on someone who is lost. Helping another in need is power in its greatest form.

Misuse of Power

Organizations run with power management hierarchies are feeling the effects of the new business "groupthink" paradigm. Groupthink involves team work, synergy and sharing responsibility. As we all have rights and freedoms, nobody wants to be bossed. Many ignorant, unknowing, "powers that be" forget this fact. I remember working on one team where the staff mentioned that this female officer was known as the "almighty" because she did not want to be challenged when she made a decision. This female authority was only fooling herself. Governments, politicians, managers and bureaucrats in positions of power often think falsely that they are the elite of society. These people are there to serve the public, hence serve us! Little do they realize that they are only deceiving themselves! Real power comes from within the individual. I have experienced bullying in my work world. School administrators and management personnel often use power control tactics. At the same time, they expect teachers to stop the bullying in the classroom and in the workplace. What a paradox. Doing unto others what we want done unto us still holds its ground.

Have you been a victim of the gossip and rumor mill? People can suggest that you not let it bother you. We, however, have to go to work on a daily basis and "live" with these people on teams, in meetings and in hallways. Being human, it does hurt. Those who gossip are often envious of others. Many do not love themselves. If we are in harmony, we have no need to negate the presence of others. Once again, it is best and it is possible, to wish these people well on their journey inward. Once realized, there is great power and freedom in personal development. Far too often, though, the temptations and defense mechanisms kick in high gear and keep people living in fear. I am certain you can name some examples.

Temptations and Corruption

The temptations to be corrupt are present on a daily basis. Having the angel on one shoulder and the devil on the other, both whispering in your ears at the same time, is an experience we all face daily. Do it or don't do it, cheat or don't cheat, tell the truth or tell a lie - the temptations are endless for everyone. We must acknowledge our dark side and accept this as part of being human. We can learn to make better choices. If we ignore our humanness, the temptations often increase and become overwhelming. While preparing us to make better decisions, accepting and admitting our weaknesses and temptations keep us humble and ethical. If we do not admit our weaknesses, they can control us.

Avoiding corruption and resisting temptation are daily challenges. Power has to be used appropriately. Political games and gains, the mismanagement of money, the misuse of people, the loss of important morals and values and, of course, destructive decisions often result when we are out of balance. The answer lies in personal development - becoming better daily by fine-tuning our lives and making better decisions. As free-thinking individuals, trust yourself.

Yes ... and No

Some people find it hard to make their own decisions. Many have become victims of institutions where the norm is to "get in" with management and do as you are told. You know the situation and the feeling it can bring. These people who "tow the line" and agree with everything are not free thinkers. If they choose to be, anyone can learn to be free.

"Yes, man", the assistant mumbles as he leaves the meeting. "Yes, maam", the employee says as she leaves the office. Have you ever been one of these people? Skipper Bruce was not. He had learned his lesson well from his father.

What is a "yes man" or a "yes maam"? Skipper Bruce warned me to never be a "yes man" and to always stand up for my rights as a free thinking citizen. I had heard his famous story from a few family members, but I wanted to hear it from the "horse's mouth". One day later in his life I asked him to tell me his story. Now that I had my license we often went for educational drives. I was always his student and this day was a powerful one.

I proceeded, "Poppy Bruce, please tell me the 'yes-man' story." With tears in his eyes, he mentioned how his father had told him, "Mike, don't be a yes man. Speak out, stand up for yourself and live out your rights and freedoms." A man over 70 years of age, Skipper Bruce became soft hearted when he remembered a story from his wise father. Taking him to visit his deceased parents at their graves in Long Harbour, I found it difficult to hold back my tears as he struggled with his words and emotions for his "Poppy and Mommy Bruce." This taught me that it is normal to cry and to show your emotions. Our emotions, like our intelligence, must also be instructed. What a strong bond between son and parents! Despite our dysfunctions, what real power does exist in love and in family.

As we drove closer to Argentia, Newfoundland, Canada, a United States Naval Base after the Second World War, Skipper Bruce went on to finish the story. Being a civilian at the Argentia, Newfoundland Naval Base, he had been working on a construction project. As was always the case, the men on the construction project elected Skipper Bruce to be foreman. He told me he always rose to the occasion and accepted gracefully to be their crew leader. The construction team knew his leadership abilities and wisdom in working with, not only, construction materials, but more importantly, with people. His actions spoke louder than his words in a day before unions were put in place to protect workers and employees from poor management decisions and power hungry bosses.

Traveling to and from work all civilians were required to stop at the U.S. Naval facility gate to check in and check out, letting the guards know their destination. The base was erected in case of war and tight security was a part of policy and procedure. Civilians were allowed, by law, once in a while, to bring liquor and cigarettes off the U.S. Naval Base. The prices were cheaper, so many of the civilian Newfoundlanders availed of this.

As usual, on his way home one particular day, Skipper Bruce stopped. His trunk and car were quickly checked by a security officer. Following this the security officer spoke to him in a rude fashion, "Hey, what ya got in your pocket there, Mac?" Skipper Bruce stopped for a moment to gather his thoughts. He assertively declared, "My name is not Mac. My name is Mike! And what's in my pocket is mine!" Because he was probably used to hearing "Yes-man, here's what's in my pocket", the arrogant security officer stood in disbelief. Yes man ... NO man! Not Skipper Bruce. Not another word was spoken. Skipper Bruce continued on his journey with another lesson learned, to be shared for the benefit of those around him.

Word traveled, as it often does, when someone takes a stand. The security people working on the base did not know Skipper Bruce well, but he received much negative scrutiny in the weeks to follow. He admitted finding it difficult to deal daily with so many ignorant people. Finally, Skipper Bruce had enough. He was right. As a free man, he told it like it was. What is in your pocket is yours in a free society and further, standing up for yourself is necessary if you really want to earn respect. Even though it can be hard to take a stand for what you believe in, do it anyway! It is YOUR life!

Going through the proper channels, he eventually went to see the captain of the U.S. naval base. Because it was not being respectfully resolved in Newfoundland, Skipper Bruce told him straight up that he was putting his job on the line and was going to go to Washington DC, to the president's office, to have this matter solved. The captain acted quickly and settled the matter with his subordinates. We all must pick our battles. From my studies and personal experience, it seems that the majority of people are afraid to take a stand for what they know is right.

Skipper Bruce would say, "With the battles you pick, make sure you fight for all the right reasons and never give up until the end." In this situation, not many would have picked a battle with the Captain of the U.S. Naval Base. Skipper Bruce's reasoning behind his decision to go to Washington DC was simple. He said, "The U.S. people are the best in the world at standing up for one's rights. An individual's freedom of rights would never be disregarded in the United States because it is serious business when violated." I got the message loud and clear. Stand up what you believe. The power lies in you. No one will do it for you. More than ever in our new world of immense change and challenge, our individual rights and freedoms must be respected, honored and utilized.

Fear Standing Alone

Standing alone is uncomfortable. Doing what is right, even though we know others will not approve, can be an ugly feeling. On the one hand, it seems many want to have the power; on the other hand, when it is time to make a serious decision they will step back and "sit on the fence". It can be linked to fear - fear of what others may think about them. What others think about you is not important. What is important is what you think about yourself.

What is fear? Many professional speakers use the acronym f.e.a.r. to stand for "false evidence appearing real" or "false education appearing real". All fear is self-created. Coinciding with fear is insecurity. The only security in today's society is risk-taking. Risk-taking often equals security-making. Why not be an independent individual and seek your own goals and dreams? Even if it does hurt, stand alone and do the right thing. Do it in fear because the only audience you ever have to please is the personal and professional audience of one – YOU!

Deal with a problem instead of hoping it will go away on its own. Problems, especially those dealing with fellow human beings, must be faced. Many of us never learn this concept growing up and some never learn it. Skipper Bruce often commented on people who would "hide behind their masks" – job titles, perceived social status, letters after their name and self-proclaimed "important people". One day at a local garage, his car had been repaired but he was not satisfied with the work completed. The reason was simple: the car was not repaired. He phoned and phoned and phoned the owner of the garage to no avail. Finally, he went to visit the owner and could not get a response. He told me that he knew the owner was in the building but was "too cowardly to come out and provide customer service." Skipper Bruce was disappointed but he stood alone and picked this battle because he was right – the problem was not fixed and he was charged for the repairs. Have you even been there? Learning to face your fears and deal with cowardly individuals takes practice. Once again, education and self-development are the answer; wisdom is acquired along the way.

Albert Einstein states: "Wisdom is not a product of schooling but of the life-long attempt to acquire it." Standing alone for what is right is what Skipper Bruce did best. He trusted his father's wisdom, not only in the schooner, but also in everyday life. This enabled him to see the bigger picture. Having solid convictions is a challenge for many of us. It is easy to become confused without education and experience. Education, over time, equals experience. Experience combined with knowledge and action, equals wisdom. Experience in business, in teaching, in government or in any area of life, does not make a person wise. Real wisdom comes from your knowledge and acting upon that knowledge, learning as much as you can along the way to craft better life decisions. Standing alone in times of uncertainty is the ultimate essence of freedom.

How Free are We?

Skipper Bruce told me the "Yes, man" story to drive home a point. His father had told him to be careful of politicians and others who want you to tow their line. To do the right thing, often, you must stand alone. "SPEAK OUT" and "Stand up for yourself". Learn to tow your own line and lead your own ship. This is real freedom.

What is freedom? It is a universal privilege of independence. We, in the Western world, live in a free society…or do we? Those of us who do not live in fear and do not believe in the status quo are probably the most free. Because people fear change, they often remain stuck in their current conditions. Maybe they do not fear change as much as they fear that things might get worse if they do change. We have the power as citizens in a free society to live the life we choose. We are as free as we make up our minds to be. Now is the time for you to choose to be free and live how you wish to live.

The greatest freedom of all, freedom of speech, comes from freedom of choice. We are free to say what we wish as long as it does not interfere with anybody else's freedom. Not enough people are educated in this regard. Our school systems do not really teach this. Some students get graded based on whether they agree or disagree with a teacher. Real education is being able to see an idea or concept from more than one angle. Then, you are able to think independently and make your own decisions, instead of having others decide how you will live.

Those with positive power must learn to "Walk lightly but carry the big stick." It takes time to get used to this idea. "Your presence," many of my friends warned, "Is threatening to anyone who is the least bit insecure." I took it as a compliment more than anything. It is now easy to remember, in vivid detail, Skipper Bruce and his "walk with the big stick." Because he stood for the common man and our beautiful natural environment, never thinking of himself any better or any worse than any human being, I often sensed that many business people in the community feared him. He loved and respected all, putting people and their happiness first. For him, all else was secondary to loving another as one would want to be loved, treated and respected. We must love people and use power/money/possessions for the benefit of all. This is where the real life power rests and we have a choice to use it or not.

Chapter 5 Nuggets for Digestion:

~ Speak out; practice your freedom of speech.
~ You really only have power and control over one person - YOU!
~ For best results, power must be shared.
~ Share your power, share your material possessions and share your life wisdom.
~ The servant (government) is not greater than its master (public citizens).
~ Those who try to rain on your parade have no parade of their own.
~ Never "tow the line"; be a free thinker and a free willed decision maker.
~ Do not be or become a "Yes Man" or a "Yes Maam."
~ Let your actions speak louder than your words.
~ Take a stand for what you believe. Pick your battles.
~ When necessary, stand alone.
~ Fear means False EVERYTHING Appearing Real.
~ Learn wisdom, not just knowledge.
~ You are as free as you make up your mind to be.
~ Walk lightly but carry a big stick.
~ Love people and use power.
~ The time is now to be FREE!

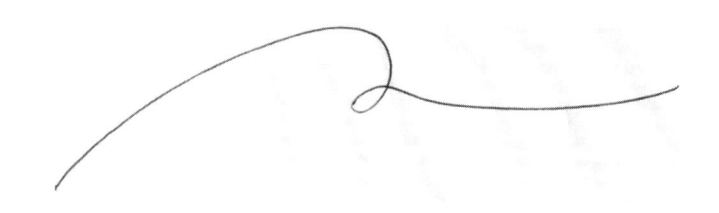

6

The First Two P's of Life Leadership

The real ship you are leading is a ship called YOURSELF.
Skipper Michael Joseph Bruce

Leadership is helping people see themselves in a more positive light. Real leaders have strong morals and values. They help people with matters of the heart, not just matters of the mind. Skipper Bruce not only talked about the leadership principles of life, he lived them. Real life leadership, he believed, is all about you.

P# 1: Boy Scout Philosophy - <u>Preparation</u>

The Boy Scout motto, "Always be prepared", serves us well in our self-leadership quest. Life is full of twists and turns, ups and downs, high points and low points. Where possible, we must be ready to meet these challenges. In Newfoundland and Labrador, and other places on the Atlantic seaboard, there is much fog created from the offshore collision of warm and cold ocean currents. One must be thoroughly prepared. Skipper Bruce, who always took a compass, learned this on the schooner with his father and he applied it to our outdoor adventures. We never know what can happen in life. Skipper Bruce's back-up plans prepared us to face many challenges.

On one ice fishing adventure, I surprised myself. Skipper Bruce always enjoyed the boiled kettle with hot tea to go with our home made lunches. It was a challenge, sometimes, to get the fire burning quickly. The woods, on this particular day, were soaking wet as it had rained the previous night. The cold winter frost had set in that morning and the ram-pikes had frozen. I, however, was prepared! I had taken some extra paper, dry kindling and a home-made paraffin wax fire starter that my father and I had made during a Boy Scouts' overnight.

At noon, Skipper Bruce continued to fish through the ice as I broke away to prepare the lunch. Setting up the base for the fire, I was now ready. The kindling caught but was quickly extinguished by the dripping moisture coming from the frosty wood. The fire starter still had a small flame coming from its centre, so I quickly built up some of the back up kindling on the base of the flame. Once again it ignited. Once again it extinguished quickly. After five attempts, all supplies, except for some spare newspaper I had put in Skipper Bruce's packsack, were gone.

Having rebuilt the base of the fire, I placed down this last piece of newspaper. Just as I had hoped, the frosty sticks and twigs had now become dry. Feeding the embers some fresh oxygen, I leaned in and gave it my best breath. After two minutes of huffing and puffing, the fire came alive. Warm feet and a hot cup of tea was ours. Skipper Bruce and fellow ice fishermen were amazed. Mental preparation was an important piece of this victory. We must always be prepared to face life's daily challenges.

Failing to plan is planning to fail. Writing your plans on paper helps ensure that you will follow through. Prepare well in advance with backup plans. Expect the unexpected. With plans to follow, the little disappointments that occur day to day do not have the power to overwhelm us.

The power of a list, in preparing, as well as in goal setting, cannot be overlooked. In preparing for some major fishing trips, I will list fishing supplies in one column, food and medical supplies in another column, camping supplies in another and miscellaneous items in another. Keeping a journal is also useful. Documenting lessons learned and ideas that come to mind for life, career, business, relationships and overall success is valuable. At a recent speaker's meeting, one of our professional speakers told the story of the great idea he and a colleague had. Driving home from a workshop they had conducted, the idea mysteriously appeared in conversation. When they got home to discuss it further, the idea had vanished just as quickly as it had spawned. The lesson is simple: our minds are so busy sometimes that we easily forget. Never trust your memory with important information. Write things down.

Fine Tuning Preparation

In times of need and in times of least expectation, we often require extra supplies. We would all agree that it is better to have extra money than not enough or ample health than not enough. Having extra supplies on a fishing adventure is one way to prevent disaster. Skipper Bruce taught me this concept in the University Life and it was reinforced by my father while in the Boy Scouts. Always take extra because it is better to have too much, than not enough. A fishing buddy of mine, Robin, in Ontario told me, "As a diabetic, it is better to have the extra chocolate bars in the packsack, rather than back in the truck, especially if your sugar goes low." I, having insulin dependent, type-one diabetes, have learned this lesson over and over again. A lesson keeps being repeated until it is learned. Taking extra food and extra sugar is part of my specific routine. We must be thoroughly prepared.

Weathering Storms

One of the challenges all anglers face is that of poor weather. We never know when rain showers are going to happen or when the wind is going to blow so hard that it seems like the river is flowing upstream. In this situation, casting a fly is almost impossible. Knots in your leader, a bend in your line and a poor presentation result from heavy wind. Like Skipper Bruce would say, "That wind blows on us all at different times and we have to learn how to battle it." As the captain of *The James and Martha* schooner, he would say, "Set your life sail skillfully so that the wind does not take you where you do not wish to go." Because he was a man of the seas, I trusted his wisdom tremendously. It did take some time for me to arrive at a destination that I enjoyed. Being students of life and all its ups and downs, we all go through this.

Many of us get lost when we leave high school or when we leave post-secondary institutions. It becomes overwhelming. We often do not know where to begin. Trying to set your sail in a societal hurricane is not only challenging but emotionally tiresome. The key, of course, is to set your sail skillfully. While you try to move through life, set it solidly like a rock, so that the winds of despair and negativity do not crash your ship.

Prepare to Pay Attention

My old high school basketball coach constantly reminded me to "pay attention" as my mind wandered while playing on the court. On a number of occasions, he singled me out to set an example for the others to pay attention to the play and what was happening around our playing "zone." "Pay attention" are two simple, yet powerful, words. Observation helps in the preparation process. Plans change, we change, business changes, people's wants and needs change, and life changes regularly. We must be prepared to meet these changes.

We must also pay attention to the strange signs that we receive. Last summer, my father set up a rodent trap, to catch the pesky squirrels that were eating the bird seed on the feeder. He caught quite a few and then drove out of town where he released them into the wild. On one occasion, he had trouble getting the squirrel out of the box. Dad shook it and shook it, to no avail. The squirrel was frightened and clung to the opposite side of the box. Dad put his hand in the box to give the squirrel a nudge and grabbed the squirrel by the tail. The squirrel would not move, but Dad's hand did. He removed the tip of the squirrel's tail, as it bolted out of the box and into the woods! Mission accomplished and a small piece of squirrel tail as evidence of the story.

On a visit with my parents, I heard this remarkable story. Dad handed me the squirrel tail, knowing that I make artificial flies for fishing, and he said, "Here, make me a squirrel bug that floats." I made him a unique dry-fly, one that sits high on the water. In our next two days of salmon fishing on the river, no flies were working. Dad put on his "squirrel tail" bug. He lost two (one was a large 10 pound fish) salmon the first day and retained two the second day. His tags were filled. Dad commented, "Another successful salmon season down; here, put it all away 'til next year." We do not know how our plans and life will change with short notice. Paying attention to the mysterious, comical things can simultaneously make a difference, and be fun.

We must also leave room for adjustment. In the field of construction and the profession of engineering, ample thought and preparation solves serious problems. Roads rerouted, bridges designed with different infrastructure, buildings and parking lots are changed to better meet land requirements. Problem solving is much easier, and often less stressful, when we are prepared. Good preparation involves consistent focus and seeing oneself successful in advance. This will ensure results.

Results are what we seek. Concentration and focus are necessary. Oftentimes, attention to detail is required. This lesson came to me the hard way, as usual. I kept rising a big salmon one afternoon and wondered why I could not hook her. Cast after cast, she came savagely to the fly. I kept missing her. I knew that something was up so I took in my fly and discovered the hook was snapped off. On the back-cast, I had hit the cliff behind me. After I changed my fly, the fish was no longer willing to take the offering or, more likely, she had moved on.

Paying attention to details is crucial not only in fishing but in day-to-day living. The details create the excitement and we must be careful to focus. Many times, I have rose fish when I least expected it. When you are not having any success for several hours, it is often hard to keep concentrating on your fly. It appears that the moment you are not ready, the fish is. In watching veteran anglers, I have realized that they rarely take their eyes off the fly. They can see the fly at all times no matter how far or how near the fly is from them. This certainly is a skill that requires practice, focus, concentration and sound preparation. It pays off.

Adequate preparation and observation from past successes and failures is a starting point for the life leadership challenge. Can we always be prepared? No! We, however, can be as prepared as possible. How are you preparing your life leadership journey in this world of change? Now is the time for a readjustment in your leadership philosophy. In the words of *Nike*, "Just do it!"

P #2: **Presentation**

Everyone presents. Going on a date, participating in a job interview, selling a product, making or receiving an offer on a house, speaking at a meeting, teaching, shopping for groceries, fishing - all are presentations. Whether we realize it or not, we are all always presenting. Thus, we are all into sales. How do you sell yourself when you present?

In public, we are often judged by how we look. While we wish this was not the case, it is reality. When I went to high school, all male teachers wore dress shirts and ties, while the female teachers always wore their best "dressy" outfits for the job. Has casual dress taken over? It is true that the external appearance of an individual sometimes reflects the internal thoughts and feelings that one possesses. From a cognitive therapy standpoint this makes sense. Those who are the most successful in their chosen professions and careers always look their best and present themselves in ways that command respect.

My friend, who owns a formal wear business, is correct. He says, "ALWAYS look your best and dress like a million bucks" - even if you do not own a million dollars. He means this as a form of self-respect. Whether we go to the grocery store, to the theatre or to work, we must dress our best. Many women are experts at the dressing game. Men can learn this as well. Be natural, of course, but always present your best.

Natural Presentations

In the field of human nature and the psychology of life, we know that results mean everything. Intending to produce something does not take us far. Presenting to produce results is where we all stand. When I first started fly fishing for Atlantic salmon, I invested many long hours with little results. My fly presentation was not natural. It seems that the Atlantic salmon prefers a natural floating fly, one that best moves with the flow of the stream. Learning to present the fly naturally was a challenge for me. I had learned the correct mechanics of fly casting but not the mechanics of letting nature do the work of my fly in the stream. That is why some fishermen catch more fish than others. They understand that life is a natural process and the fly should be presented naturally to the fish - for best results.

Presentation is **everything** in Atlantic salmon fishing. How the fish perceives the fly is what matters most in Atlantic salmon fishing success. Trout, on the other hand, take the fly for feeding purposes. Nobody knows why the Atlantic salmon takes the fly. Presenting your fly perfectly to a salmon is an art and a science. The fish waits patiently for the perfect pass of the fly above its lie in the water before striking. If what you do with your fly is not perfect, your results will usually reflect this error in presentation. It makes logical sense.

On one fishing trip to the Pinware River, I rose a fish and pulled the fly away before she could grab it. My buddy, not having much luck, was nearby and I offered him a cast. He flicked his fly on top of the fish, but nothing. He flicked the fly behind the fish, above the fish, to the side of the fish. The salmon did not return. My friend gave up. I knew his presentation was wrong and told him so. He stepped back. Having given the fish about 60 seconds to rest from seeing any of our flies on the water, I flicked my fly up and away from the fish. Mother Nature was now in command. She took the fly gracefully and, as it skittered through the eddies off of the main current, it came to rest in a natural presentation right above where I knew the fish was laying. BANG! The fish inhaled the offering on the first cast and my buddy landed that fish. It is all in the presentation and how the fish perceives your fly.

Daily Presentations

Presentation makes all the difference in Atlantic salmon fishing and in life. Ask the top sales people in any field their secret to selling and they will tell you that they learned to present the product in such a way that the customer could not refuse. In our everyday lives, as well, presentation is a major aspect. How do you present yourself at a meeting? How do you present yourself to your family? How do you present yourself on a romantic date? How do you present yourself in business? It is not that people are watching that matters. When we look our best, we often feel our best. Feeling our best, we then present ourselves more naturally. Never wear you best suit tomorrow when you can wear it today. Present your best always and you will not only feel at your best, but you will attract things and circumstances that you never thought possible.

Presenting your best naturally in the workforce, in school, in society and to your friends and family can be a challenging task. Many people wear masks, afraid to present themselves for who they are - a sad fact of life. Skipper Bruce told me that there would always be people better off and worse off than you, so it is best not to compare yourself with anybody else. How wise he was! The "Hollywood Syndrome" to look like, act like and be like someone else has swept the world. These people are no different from you or me. They may be doing better, financially, but they are no better as human beings.

While celebrities seem to be living exceptional lives, many of them struggle with presenting themselves naturally. Problems with self-image, self-esteem and the ability to be themselves have affected the lives of many of society's "reality stars". Counselor colleagues who have worked with many of our current celebrities often say that it is only a fantasy world and many, if given the chance, would prefer to live a normal life away from the flash and glamour. Do you present yourself naturally or do you wish to be like someone else? You are who you are. Take your uniqueness and make the most of your life presentations.

Presentation is a daily affair. How we look and dress, how we talk and associate with other people and how we get through the day all comes down to presentation. Even those employees locked away in a cubicle still have to present themselves daily. A small shift in presentation can have a compound effect on the results produced. Ask any man who has ever tried to date a girl for the second time. The key is to make her the center of the conversation. This shift in presentation skills can alter your success rate in any situation requiring more effective communication. Ask questions and the answers will take care of themselves. Further presentation changes may include reading a book to improve your knowledge base or joining a gym to help improve your health. Your presentation will determine what you bring into your life.

Attracting Results

Some believe that the law of attraction is the number one law of life because we inevitably attract what we put out. So if we put out negative energy, envy, jealousy and all other undesirable traits, guess what we get back? The same! Fly fishing helped me realize that I had to learn to lure the fish to me. To become an avid and successful salmon angler, I had to get better at attracting fish.

Attracting Atlantic salmon to your fly is not an easy task. The challenge, however, is what makes it worthwhile. How you present the fly to the fish determines your success rate. This corresponds to any domain or chosen career. We start off slowly, but once our knowledge and experience increase over time, our results get better. The philosophy of personal development allows us to attract better things. What have you attracted up to this point from your life presentations?

Presentation is the major determinant of salmon fishing success. Those who learn to work with Mother Nature and the laws of the river current achieve the best success. How many people in life try to work against reality? I used to be one of these people blaming the government, blaming my negative relatives, blaming my neighbor (wishing they would move!), blaming my girlfriend, blaming anything and everything for my unhappy life situation. Eventually, I realized that it was "I" who had to attract better outcomes. It was "I" who either brought home the salmon or did not. I was responsible for my presentations in life. When I changed, everything changed. It all started with going to work on me and my daily presentations.

Self-Belief and Style

Self-esteem and self-image are what matter most for human beings. Our external presentations are often a reflection of our internal presentations. Self-esteem, or that deep down belief in yourself, no matter who you are, what you look like, what you earn, where you go to school, who your parents are, and what you think about only touches your constant audience of one - you. Skipper Bruce never had to speak about the concept of self-esteem. He possessed it. It is the one phenomenon I would love to be able to give to every human being on the planet. The deep down belief in oneself that "I am special, I am excellent, I am worth it and I like me for who I am" would make a significant difference in this world. Once again, the daily decisions we make either add to or take from our esteem accounts. Believing in you for who you are as a human being is tough, at the best of times, but it is necessary for life change to happen.

In salmon fishing, my success rate increased when my belief in my abilities increased. Was it a consequence of personal development? Did self-belief come before the number of salmon captured increased or after? Logically, we can reason, that once you achieve something, your self-esteem will increase. On the other hand, in psychology, we know that you will achieve something once your belief in self increases. This presents another great debate for the scholars. Both achievement and self-belief are intertwined. Sport psychologists claim that performance always follows belief in self because everything evolves from the inside to the outside. Thus, we first believe we are worthy and capable and then we make it happen. In your future life leadership presentations, first and foremost, believe that you can do it; then, go to work to make it happen.

Our style of presenting is a determining factor in self-leadership. How we present ourselves to the organization, to the public and to our families and friends determines the results we get. When you present, what do people first see? YOU! A successful person walks confidently and acts confidently. Even if you struggle with self-esteem and self-confidence, present yourself in the same manner. Sometimes we must do what is necessary, even if we struggle believing that we can do it.

Final Presentation Thoughts

"Thinking is the hardest work there is, which is the probable reason that so few engage in it", as Henry Ford stated. Skipper Bruce always commented, "Who cares what anyone else thinks as long as you do your best?!" His wise words are so true in a society paralyzed by fear. It is amazing how so many people are afraid to go in public for fear of being judged. A powerful concept in cognitive therapy includes these three ideas:

1. Very few people think!
2. Those that do think are certainly not thinking about you!
3. Even if they do think about you, their thinking will not have any affect on you…unless you allow it to happen!

The power is in your response. So stay in command of your life and, as much as possible, think positive thoughts. As self-centered creatures, whether we realize it or not, the majority of people are concerned with how they present themselves in public. They are not concerned about you or anyone else. Present yourself well and focus on what you want. This will reflect positive self-esteem which will attract, in turn, the right things to you. Genuine life leadership is all about how you present yourself to others and to life. How do you present yourself daily?

Chapter 6 Nuggets for Digestion:

~ P #1 for Life Leadership: Be Prepared…<u>ALWAYS!</u>
~ Leadership is about helping people help themselves become better.
~ Never fail to plan.
~ Write your plans, goals and dreams on paper.
~ Keep a journal of life leadership ideas; do not trust your memory.
~ Expect the unexpected.
~ It is better to have too much than not enough.
~ Learn to set your sail wisely.
~ We are always presenting; present naturally.
~ Always dress your best.
~ Small daily presentation changes yield major long-term results.
~ Become better at "attracting fish" in your life.
~ We are responsible for our life presentations.
~ You are EXCELLENT and worth it!
~ Build up your self-esteem and self-love tanks daily.
~ Your success rate increases in direct proportion to your increase in self-esteem.
~ Performance will always follow your belief in yourself.
~ P #2 for Life Leadership: Presentation. Present yourself well!

7

The Final Two P's of Life Leadership

It takes twenty years to make an overnight success.
Eddie Cantor

P #3: Have <u>Patience</u>

Skipper Bruce epitomized the word "patience" in his daily actions. Growing up a spiritual, not necessarily religious man, he believed that all good things come to those who wait. Whether casting for salmon on the river or fixing a leaky faucet in his home, without complaint or frustration, he practiced patience.

Skipper Bruce's actions spoke louder than his wise words. On the Salmon River, I watched him cast and cast and cast with little or no success. I adopted this philosophy of having patience without complaint. My only dilemma was that I did not know why I adopted it. I remember going with Skipper Bruce to fix a series of leaky pipes in a house in the local community. In order to save money, the previous plumbing crew had obviously taken the easy route in the construction phase of the house. The owner of the house now had serious trouble. Even though, I was five years old at the time, I recall vividly Skipper Bruce taking his time on the project while getting it done correctly. With his booming educational voice he said to me, "If the job is worth doing, it is worth doing right." If your life project is worth doing, it is worth doing correctly.

Patience is a foundational tool for life leadership success. Even though a student's university degree takes four years, requiring much hard work, the student can not speed up the process of those four years. Enjoying the four years to completion, with all its highs and lows, may lead to experiences not possible if one is impatient. Maybe this is why the phrase, "Life is a journey, not a destination" makes sense. It is a gentle reminder that once a time frame is up, another time frame will take its place. Thus, we must be patient and enjoy the journey to better life experiences. Who knows when your life changing idea will come? I hope it comes from this book.

In any new adventure we undertake, the lifelong learning curve is steep. Every real life winner that we know started off as a beginner and got better with practice, feedback, and continuous learning. Far too many people beginning a new road of life, such as joining a gym, taking a class, starting a business or entering a new relationship, lose patience in the process. Have you been there? People often want immediate gratification and instant results. This is not a philosophy for long-term happiness and success. We cannot rush the passing of time. Patience helps us develop solid character. First, we must plant new seeds. Later, when the time is right, we shall reap the new results.

The teacher, student, construction worker, parent, and fly fishing angler - all must have patience. We cannot change this law of life. In all things, Skipper Bruce advised, "Take your time in whatever you do." Particularly in our fast paced world, how correct he was. Patience can be a difficult skill to master. It can, however, be learned!

Due Season

Once the season is right, the harvest is ready. A farmer cannot pick a crop in the summer because it is not the correct season - the plant has not fully grown and developed. Thus, the farmer must be patient, until the season of fall arrives. If your preparation is complete and you have learned the concept of patience, positive results will soon follow. As an individual who thinks "outside the box", I had overlooked a very important piece of my life puzzle. Through personal choice and many decisions that I had not realized I had made, I had boxed myself into a system where I was not meant to be. While on the inside looking out, it is hard to see the dirt on the outside of the glass. Maybe you are in a life situation where you are not meant to be?

The truth does set us free. Impatience can lead to greed and bad decision making. Being impatient, at the time, I once made a very life changing decision to chase a Math teaching position that I did not really want. I was trained to teach high school Biology and Physical & Health Education. What a learning experience this was! When all of my teaching colleagues had positions in September, it appeared that I did not want to be left out. At the time, I lacked the self-discipline and the ability to relax and think about what I was doing. I made a "snap decision" and I took the job without weighing the pros and cons. In the end, it was a great learning experience.

Making snap decisions can be costly, so make your choices wisely. Being spontaneous can be great, but self-educated decision making will help us think our decisions through before we decide on major life challenges and changes. Being human, many times we do learn from our mistakes. Skipper Bruce knew how much the experiences of life can teach us. With time and patience, it is necessary to push through life's troubles to arrive at better destinations. It hurts, but nothing worth achieving in life is without some pain.

This Too Shall Pass

"This, too, shall pass" is an expression I have heard during some of my deepest moments of pain and despair. A term used in counseling, it reinforces the idea, that with due time, things will improve. Sometimes improvement is the only option. We may feel that things cannot get any worse. We could all use a gentle reminder about time and patience during our hardest moments of suffering.

Not knowing what it was, I had gone through a clinical depression several times. As one can expect, I was somewhat impatient. Because I did not take care of my health, I was my own worst enemy. Have you ever been down this road of self-discovery? Depression is a stress-related illness. It can be metabolic (internal; genetically related) or situational (external; life-events based). Once again the law of sowing and reaping or the science of action and reaction take affect. As I have discovered, for every result, there is a cause. Not taking care of myself and not knowing how to handle stress put me in the right position to experience some of life's lowest moments. We often must hit "rock bottom" before we can change and get better. Being weak allows us to eventually understand what it means to be strong and healthy.

While in a state of depression, it is difficult to be patient. The depressed state does not creep up overnight and, thus, will not disappear overnight. With the passing of time, however, it does disappear. Have you ever been through a clinical depression? Sometimes we need to experience difficult times to give us greater perspective and wisdom. With patience, we can see both the positive and negative sides. Anyone who has been down the dark journey of stress, depression, and despair, must always remember that "This too shall pass." When we make better choices and learn to handle the tests thrown upon us, it always does.

Testing Patience

Fly fishing for Atlantic salmon is the ultimate test of one's patience. As fish captured are what we strive for, cast after cast, with no results can tantalize even the most patient person. I remember one gentleman at the tidal pool on the Pinware River. He was raising a fish, time after time, but could not hook the fish and secure a battle. As I walked up the river bank, I stopped to watch as his long cast swung perfectly into the path of the curling salmon. I did notice that he was making the same mistake as I had made. "Give the fish an extra second before you lift", I said. He heeded my advice on the next cast and within five minutes, he had played and landed the fish. As I walked up the river, he shouted, "Thank you!" We often learn best by teaching because it reinforces concepts already learned.

After many years of struggle, one experience on the Pinware River in Labrador revealed to me that I had finally learned patience. On this particular day, the water levels were low. There were numerous fish in the river, but they were not being caught. The wind was blowing a gale and I proceeded to go down over the bank below the bridge to a pool called, "The Bathtub." As I did not want to scare any fish that might have been resting, I stayed back, out of view to the pool, and climbed carefully down the cliff like a mountain goat. In high water, anglers just walk directly to the big rock as they are not concerned about spooking any fish.

I observed Mother Nature's conditions and planned my attack. I figured the fish were lying in the tail end of the pool where the oxygen concentration was high. My very first cast went perfectly over a little water ripple where the water emptied from the main pool. As my wet fly swung into the main current, I could see a thick salmon rise underneath the fly in curiosity. One rise and I was excited! The wind, however, picked up instantly and I could not cast correctly. It did not dissipate. Because it did not land perfectly, I cast back again and hauled the fly out of the water. I knew my presentation now had to be perfect in such low water conditions or I would "mess up the pool".

Having played this patience game many times before, I refused to quit. As I knew that the fish was interested and that it had not been spooked, I checked my fly. The leader was securely attached and it drifted across the water perfectly. I made a simple cast near my feet to check the angle of the fly coming across the river from the side where I was fishing.

The wind once again played havoc and blew the fly upstream! Now, as this was the last day of my trip and I only had one salmon tagged, I had to practice patience. The other tag was empty. With the extended family home for a visit to remember Skipper Bruce who had passed away one year earlier, I knew my mother wanted another fish. Now I had to practice his philosophy and deliver.

Battling the wind and water current, to get the fly exactly where I had placed it the first time, I made 12 false casts. A false cast is a cast where the angler does not present the fly on the water but keeps it in mid air, to dry it off or to perfect its landing position in the river. I was patient and waited a few minutes for the wind to relax. It did. I quietly said to myself, "I'll get you this time."

My next cast was perfect. In mid air, the blue charm fly battled the prevailing wind blowing upstream and it landed perfectly in the slow-moving current, where I had projected it to land. It swung gracefully by the side of the big rock out into the open current in the tail end of the pool, where the water emptied over the side of the "bathtub." As soon as the blue charm passed over the same salmon lie, "Whomp"! The fish nailed it and the hook was securely set. "Fish on" I yelled to myself, in a silent affirmation of achievement! After a few jumps and a solid battle, I knew the hook was secured in its jaw. Not wanting to lose this fish, I played it assertively, yet patiently.

In case I made a mistake and the fish escaped, it would have survived because I do not let them stay too long on the end of my line. We have all felt the effect of hard exercise and the build up of lactic acid in our bodies. For a fish, it takes two or three days later for the acid to diffuse. Low water in a river means less oxygen for the fish to breathe, so sometimes, the fish will die two or three days later. The catch-and-release debate has, and will continue to be, a heated controversy. Who really knows what happens in Mother Nature and we never know how many salmon die from being hooked and released. I rarely see a dead salmon on the river banks. With the vast assortment of hungry animals in nature, life and death takes care of itself.

After a solid fight, finally, the fish came to shore. Being patient I was also being cautious; this was my last chance to fill the last tag. I grabbed it securely by the gills, gave thanks as Skipper Bruce always did, tagged and cleaned the fish and went back to my car, with another victory in life lessons learned. Near the road were two American tourists. As they had witnessed several anglers with no catch, we chatted about my "luck", as fish were scarce, or so it seemed. I told them my story of patience and they agreed.

"All good things come to those who wait", is an adage paramount for life leadership. Relationships, finances, health and all the treasures in life rely on the notion that they cannot be unlearned and fixed overnight. Our decisions for betterment can change in an instant, but patience is required to fulfill what we wish to acquire. Ideal self leadership also requires the fourth P, persistence.

P #4: **<u>Persistence</u>**

There are no failures in life, unless we believe in failure. We learn lessons, yes. We, however, never really fail. Many people have not accepted this fact and have given up on their possibilities and future dreams. Even though I was giving up on my own dreams in the school system, I was one to preach this idea. When I reflected on my experience as a salmon angler, I could see how persistence kept me going forward. After five summers of fly-fishing, I improved as an angler. In all life areas, once we get better, our results get better. Once we are determined, nothing is impossible. Quitters never win and, more importantly, winners never quit.

Quitting has a negative effect on self-esteem. When we give up on something we desire, it seems to erode all of our hopes and dreams of achievement. When we believe in ourselves there can be no such thing as failure. Skipper Bruce kept reminding me, "You will get one yet. You will get one. Keep trying." This constant reinforcement helped develop my belief in my abilities. The results were a reflection of the power of words. In the second five-year block of my salmon fishing career, I did land one - and another and another and another.

Incredible results can happen with a new approach. I focused my attention on the little things that mattered - the angle of my fly coming across the current, waiting the extra second before lifting the rod, waiting for the fly to disappear before lifting the rod and setting the hook, and, of course, being prepared at all times for any possible situation. This also meant studying my craft to perfect it. In doing so, I studied others, the ways and means of Mother Nature and, of course, I reviewed Skipper Bruce's wisdom filled philosophies.

Dr. Tony Simmonds, one of my former professors at Memorial University, said that everyone needs some life coaching at some point because the complexity of life does not allow us to see everything. Listening to my mentors, Skipper Bruce especially, I did not stop trying. I refused to give up until there was salmon on the table to be eaten. To become a better fly-fisherman with a better attitude took several years. My new approach to never stop trying was the foundational philosophy that helped me become, not only a better fly-fisherman, but also a better person. Are you paying attention to things that matter in your life? Keep at it!

Change Results

Change, one thing we can be certain about, must be embraced. If we keep doing the same things hoping for better results, we are only fooling ourselves. If a different result is needed, a new approach is required. If someone is on the verge of bankruptcy and maintains their current economic habits, it is safe to bet that they will become bankrupt. If another individual is about to have a heart attack, with their current eating and lifestyle habits, and they do not change, we can anticipate the heart attack happening.

Change is powerful. While fly-fishing I persisted; but, in those early years, I persisted with the same approach. When I changed my approach and presentation, my results improved. When I became a better business person, I got better financial results. If I did not change my approach, it would not have happened for me. Likewise, if you do not change your approach, it will not happen for you.

Pain and pleasure are two driving forces behind human behavior. Overcoming procrastination is a challenge for many people. Before writing this book, I procrastinated on numerous occasions. I thought about going back to where I did not want to work. I thought about having to move away again. The pain of my past experiences and of the struggles I went through taught me not to repeat those mistakes. The pleasure of helping as many people as I can and of launching my new career as a personal development speaker and counselor excited me. When I changed, everything changed!

Results are what we seek. Until our desired results are achieved, we must persist and we must make all the necessary adjustments. With some simple modifications and lifelong learning practices, life can change dramatically. Another change I needed was one concerning my health. I could not expect my bad habits not to affect my health. In the beginning, to stop going for a beer with the boys on Friday night or to stop watching television took self-discipline. These changes have paid off. Bad habits must be replaced with better habits. Going to *Chapters* to read a book, for example, replaced going to a bar. If I was not a vibrant healthy individual, I would not be able to indulge in the love of Mother Nature and fly-fishing. Painting the picture in my mind of being too sick to enjoy life gave me the wake-up call I needed. What do you need to change today to make your life better? How must you modify your lifestyle?

Choosing to take a new approach is a challenge for many of us because we feel stuck in our past conditioning. The past, as Skipper Bruce often said, teaches us how to perform better. Let us use it wisely. Persistence tells us that if we do not get the results we desire, we must change. For some readers, the persistent daily changes will make you rich; for others, some drastic improvements in health and vitality will occur. The first fundamental involves decision.

Once we decide to make a new shift, and persistently work at it, we are on the road to a better future. I lived it. What a gamble in 2004, when I left Ontario, packed up everything, and came back to university to finish what I had once started - a master's degree in counseling psychology. This decision, not only provided more career opportunities, but also taught me more about myself and about what I was looking for in life. When possible, stay in school!

I had to reflect on the past in order to plan the future. The simple decision to act allowed everything to happen. When you look back on your life, there will be things in it that you do not wish to remember. Deciding to make the required changes is where your new life starts. Change takes time; but, with persistence and action change will happen.

Because we are catalysts of energy, life only changes when we change. Train yourself to see the end result in advance. Bite off small pieces of a major project. Keep biting until it gets accomplished. From Skipper Bruce and from my day-to-day experiences, I learned to approach life's obstacles - one chunk at a time. Major projects get accomplished one bite at a time.

The action approach is what many of the super successful business, family and societal leaders claim has made them who they are today. Many of these people do not have high school graduation or any number of letters after their names. They do have a persistent drive to never quit, until results are achieved. Adopt this approach in your new personal philosophy.

The satisfaction of achievement is incredible. Your success is not about anyone else. It is about you and what you want out of life. The powers to choose, to act, and to persist are often taken for granted. Your future success depends on you and you alone. Practice persistence and keep practicing until your new habit of choice is mastered.

Following through is a powerful persistence concept. The sales associate, who follows through after the sale and asks for referrals, is often rewarded. The loving parent, who follows through on the promises to a child, is rewarded when that child becomes a contributing member to society. Why not take on a new habit of persistence? Learn more, discover more and achieve more. "Nothing ventured, nothing gained", Skipper Bruce would say.

When the going gets tough, get going!

Life is tough and we must get going. Life is a battle at the best of times, but when we persist and focus on the end result, the tough elements do not put a strangle hold on our minds. In fact, the mind is where most of our battles are won or lost. How tough is your mind when facing a challenge? Skipper Bruce never backed down from a challenge, especially when sticking up for a co-worker's rights. In times when people were not treated well on his job sites, he viewed this as a time to toughen up and help out his colleagues. If only there were more people today like

Skipper Bruce, unafraid to take a stand and help out someone in a time of need. This is one of the many reasons he was always acclaimed foreman on the construction projects; when the going got tough, he got tougher. Is now a time for you to get tougher? If so do it!

Persisting with toughness is a challenge for all avid anglers. On some days the rivers are high, flooding with water; on other days, the rivers are low and rain is needed. To become competent, mental toughness means fishing in all river conditions. In order to keep going and keep growing on our journeys, no matter how difficult the situation, we must be mentally tough. While physical toughness is important, our mental strength is what matters most.

Our real learning never stops. The things you have learned yesterday will help you in today's endeavors. Certainly, a graduation certificate is required as a starting block for future career success; however, it is what you do with your knowledge, gifts and talents that reaps the rewards in life. When you discover individuals who are doing what they love and loving what they do, the discipline of perseverance is evident. They will not stop until they get what they want and need. Do not stop until you get what you want. Quitting is not an option for the persistent achiever.

Let nothing stop you!

One of the greatest conversations I ever had was with Matthew, a young student I worked with in Labrador. Matthew was riding his bike to school one cold morning, while I was walking, trying to keep the rain from drenching my clothes. The rain poured heavier as I neared the school and I hurried in order to avoid getting completely soaked. Across the road, Matthew came by on his bike and we chatted briefly while he peddled along. Near the path that took us to the school I said to him, "You don't mind riding in the rain." Matthew had taken his bike all week with the increased spring temperatures and he enjoyed the exercise. His response was a classic. Putting his head down, the ten-year-old boy spun off with determination and pride saying, "Nothing stops me!"

All I could think of was that this young student will probably be the next great success -giving motivational seminars around the world, doing whatever he wants to do no matter what happens. Amazingly we can learn from kids because they do not stop until they get what they want. Can you remember learning to ride a bike with training wheels? I remember falling down and getting back up, falling down and picking myself back up. I remember Skipper Bruce being there, along with my parents, cheering me on to succeed. After many long hours of practice and frustration, the balance finally came. Eventually the training wheels disappeared and I could now ride the bike without any assistance. Persistence pays off. Let nothing stop you in your life quest. You can do it!

Skipper Bruce taught me to keep going, to keep trying, and to keep learning. Do your best, always. Never wait for the perfect day for things to change for you. When you persist, you will eventually get the results that you desire…and far more than you could ever dream possible. Make your life a masterpiece of achievement and fulfillment.

Life goes on and so we must go on with it. Resisting change, living in the past, and wishing you were different does nothing productive, for society or for you. Keep growing and keep learning and keep discovering who you really are. In doing so, life will only get better - for you.

Chapter 7 Nuggets for Digestion:

~ P #3 for Life Leadership: Be Patient in everything you do.
~ A job worth doing is worth doing correctly.
~ Let your actions speak louder than your words.
~ We cannot rush the passing of time so enjoy all of life's moments.
~ Every winner started out as a beginner.
~ Short term pain = long term gain.
~ Practice delaying gratification. "This too shall pass."
~ We all reap rewards in due season.
~ We never know strength until we have felt weakness.
~ Problems usually don't happen instantly; neither do solutions.
~ There are no failures in life unless you believe there are.
~ Winners never quit!
~ We all need help sometimes.
~ Change your approach to change your desired result.
~ The past is a learning tool to teach us how to do better.
~ Choose to ACT!
~ Approach life's obstacles and projects one chunk at a time.
~ Follow through on what you say you will do.
~ Life is tough at the best of times, so toughen up-mentally.
~ "Nothing ventured, nothing gained."
~ P #4 for Life Leadership: Persist! Never stop until you get what you desire.

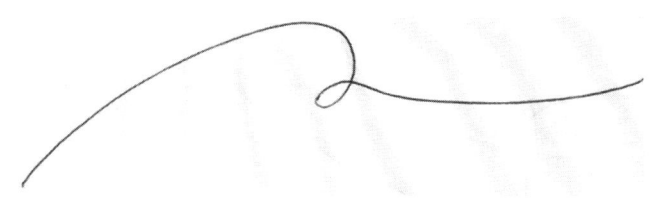

8

Majoring in MAJOR Life Areas

We can have more than we've got because we can become more than we are.
Jim Rohn

All students of life must major in the life subject of self-education or personal development. Formal education, according to America's foremost business philosopher, Mr. Jim Rohn, will help you get a job. Self-education will help make you rich - in health, in professional and personal relationships, in finances, and in spiritual matters.

Self-education is what separates those who do and those who do not. Identifying your inborn talents, initiating and continuing your personal development, and seeing what you can do to design a winning lifestyle is the real challenge. To evaluate student placement on the norm in formal educational settings, we collect testing information.

Formal schooling teaches us what to think; while self-education and personal development teaches us how to think. There is a difference. Many people cannot connect the logic associated with solving a math problem to the logic of solving a life problem.

Many, who are not academically inclined, can solve life problems and, thus, make the most out of their inborn talents. One businessman I know graduated from high school and at that point, stopped his formal schooling. He worked on his carpentry trade and now operates a million dollar business. Not only did he solve his life problem of survival in a tough economy; but he found that his ability to work with people made him happy and successful. His family, his employees, and his clients recognized his talents, which, in turn, helped to build his self-esteem. This kept him going upward and onward to becoming more valuable in his life and in the lives he has affected. Further he is a family man and a community man who is well-respected. Most of his learning came from life itself and not from formal schooling.

Schooling Ideas

One colleague of mine commented that our current public education system really only prepares students for university or college. He, I think, was correct. Is that going to change? Not anytime soon. What can change is your initiative to start your own schooling process about life, about people, about success, about education, and about personal possibilities. Now is the time to start to fix your future.

The focus in public school has always been on acquiring a good education, getting a job and letting life happen. This is perfectly fine. Those with this status-quo philosophy, however, just "let life pass them by". It is personal choice. My aunt, in Ontario, explained the difference between a job and a career. Until then, I did not really understand the difference. A job is an economic necessity; while a career is a long term investment in life. What a difference! Time spent on developing a fulfilling career is far more valuable than money. Once we invest in something we enjoy, the money and security mysteriously seems to follow - a major idea to contemplate and integrate into your own lifelong learning program.

Many obstacles come our way. We are tested…daily. Some have trouble learning life lessons and never graduate to the bigger rewards. The majority of your life lessons, I am willing to bet, did not occur in a classroom, in public school, in college or in university. On the one hand, post secondary education makes considerable contributions to society with research and new knowledge; but, on the other hand, it does not prepare us for the realities of life. We need more. Human beings operate on the achievement instinct where we always want to strive for more. This is normal, and in today's knowledge-based society we need to keep learning.

Many students, for example, face student loan debt once they finish post-secondary education. School does not adequately teach us money management. Like many, I learned the hard way. We cannot rely on the government to provide finances for post- secondary education. We must rely on ourselves and study economic basics. The basics are usually always the best because they are easily remembered. We must learn the skills necessary for managing finances and staying ahead of debt from those who have made the mistakes, from books, and from people who know the answers. We must always think outside the boxes, that society has erected, to see possibilities that many fail so see.

Outside the Box

Have you ever seen the "9 Dot Exercise?" The exercise and rules are as follows:
- connect all nine dots with only four straight lines
- your pen or pencil cannot leave the page
- backtracking over a line counts as another line
- start at one dot and only draw four straight lines
- each dot must be touched by a line

(For the answer, please email Paul: pmw@paulwhite.ca but keep trying until you get it!)

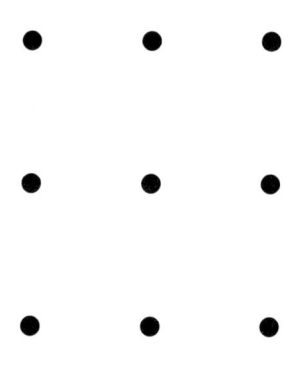

• • •

• • •

• • •

Box Theory

Box theory postulates that in society we are conditioned to think inside boundaries. Because we are used to certainty, to structure, and to knowledge of what to expect, our brains have been programmed to see only what exists - the nine dots in the shape of a box. Human beings are, however, programmed to think at a deeper level. Albert Einstein stated, "Imagination is more important than knowledge." The only boundaries that we possess are the ones that we set. Now is the time to think BIGGER and better, and to act in ways to challenge the status-quo.

At an international conference in Texas, I met Lin, a unique lady, who summarized what I had done in life. I had allowed myself to be boxed in. She suggested that I was getting thrown out of my safety box. Was it painful? Yes, indeed! Was it worth the pain? Yes, indeed! Have you ever felt boxed in? If we believe we are free to do anything we want in life, we can and will. Choose not to be boxed in. Now is the time for you to choose freedom. Pull your own strings and do not become a puppet.

Skipper Bruce often wrote letters to the editor of the paper stating his views on controversial topics. Even though he was often criticized for this, he did it anyway. In his day, the internet was not available and education was in the hands of the few. Today, education is available to anyone who wishes to jump online and seek an answer. As a counselor, I advise clients to come up with their own answers following their own research. Become a free thinker to avoid the boxes imposed by others.

Because many parents, teachers and society, in general, have our youth "boxed in", teaching students the idea of freedom has been a challenge. Only through lifelong learning and discovering the real truth can we ever escape the boxes in life that appear to have us trapped. Students often feel boxed in by the parameters of society and the "system." We were all born innocent children, with nothing, and we all end life the same way, with nothing. As adults, it is difficult to

shake past fears and inhibitions that hold us back. The suggestion that it can be overcome is difficult to believe.
People will attempt to box you in with manipulation and control. Working and associating with such people, is often a major challenge. Consider these people "tests" on the path to personal freedom and fulfillment. The goal is to become wiser in your associations and working environment. Seek out the answers to the problems and avoid people who attempt to control you.

Be assertive! "Speak out", Skipper Bruce would say. "Stand up for yourself." You have the power to change. In counseling, when a client finally accepts that s/he has the power to change and make life better, astonishing results always follow. You hold the power. Do not give it to anyone or anything. It is your life to live.

Major problems need solutions. Often thinking beyond the problem leads to understanding and resolution. The Wright Brothers did not think about staying on the ground but about flight in the air. This "unboxed" thinking eventually resulted in the beginning of a major world wide system of travel. Seeing things not yet discovered is what everyone has the potential to realize. This happens best by thinking and acting beyond the boxes of society. It is often a simple process, not requiring advanced post- secondary education.

Higher Order Thinking

Higher order thinking is not reserved for people with advanced university study. Many of the top breakthroughs and life successes that have impacted society have come from those who have not attended college or university.

These action-packed individuals create techniques to help our society in a positive, caring way.

When the student is set, the teacher will be met. Whether the teacher is a friend, a relative or a life lesson from a horrible experience, such is often the case. Instruction comes from many bizarre, yet powerful, sources of education. Mentoring is powerful! Many times, people with more wisdom and life experience can see our situations from a different perspective. We must be cautious though as free advice is often meaningless. Some people will go out of their way to try to teach others lessons and share what they think they know while many people do not ask for help. You have witnessed this. Free advice is often free because it is not worth anything. As a friend of mine once said "If I wanted advice, I would pay for it." Considering the idea of the student being ready for the teacher, his point is valid.

One evening on the River of Ponds, I fished quietly to myself, minding my own business. I was the only angler on the left side of the river facing the first pond. After fishing close to shore, I proceeded to wade out into the river and cast my fly to the middle of the pool where I had seen salmon jumping. They were moving up the river. Sure enough, I had action around my fly, but I could not entice the salmon to inhale my floating fly. A local guide walked down the opposite side of the river with his party of anglers, on their way back to camp. He stopped and attempted to make a scene of me as I stood and fished where I had rose fish.

The *expert* yelled at me saying, "YOU'RE STANDING IN THE MIDDLE OF THE POOL!"

I made the mistake of entertaining his conversation when in fact I should have ignored such "free advice", after having fished this river for many seasons.

After looking around, seeing no one on my side of the river I replied, "There is no one fishing over here."

"How can they, with you standing in the pool?" was his response. I fished patiently trying to concentrate on my fly as this distraction lingered.

Upon leaving, he blurted out, "You're standing where there's more salmon than you'll ever hook in a lifetime." Amazing! What a great guide and teacher, I thought to myself as I continued to fish where I wanted to fish. Then he proceeded to teach an older man how to fish as the older man and his wife were trying to enjoy the beauty and peacefulness of the atmosphere. Many self-proclaimed experts could use some higher order thinking. There is a right way and a wrong way to teach and help people. Free advice is usually not worth anything. Cooperative teaching and learning is the best approach, but only when the student is ready.

Cooperation and Competition

Competition, necessary to keep people striving for more, is everywhere. Is it better to be more cooperative in our approach to living? Competition seems to cause grief, start wars, and perpetuate violence. Even though it can be entertaining, as in professional sports, it does more damage to the human psyche than we will ever understand.

Cooperating and sharing is a higher order skill. It is much better to share the river, share the pools, share the tips and even share the fish. On the River of Ponds with the "Salmon Man", Ivan Payne, we helped a young boy land his first salmon. Ivan was coaching the young boy in the low water conditions, as I fished down below "Matty's Shoal", closer to where the ocean emptied into the sea. When Ivan helped him improve his cast, a salmon rose. The fish rose several times, but the young boy was taking the fly away from the fish before the fly was in its mouth.

After a few misses, I sang out, "Give the fish an extra second." Ivan agreed and, as he stepped back, the fish rose again. This time the young boy waited. A few seconds later, with my heart now pounding, I told him, "Okay, lift!" The scene was incredible! The rod bent over as the young boy made a solid connection. His reel started to wail! Now hooked, the fish headed straight for the ocean. Ivan coached him in playing the salmon out. A solid battle that lasted for five minutes seemed like an eternity. When the fish tired and came close enough to shore, I grabbed it by the gills. Team work had paid off. Helping this young angler was more thrilling than hooking the fish myself. Skipper Bruce was correct once again: "Helping other people out is what life is really all about." Altruism is not only higher order thinking and living, but also it is a win-win philosophy for happiness and fulfillment.

Real Life Success

Many philosophers claim that the universal law of attraction is the ultimate law of life. Rhonda Byrne's "Secret" has swept the world. The "Secret" is not a secret at all. It has been around for centuries and well-documented. The problem is that people did not know how to use it correctly. Some say that it is nothing but the power of positive thinking. They are partially correct; but it has more to do with the power of "positive becoming" than anything else. "Success is something you attract by the person you become", says Jim Rohn. We attract that which we give out. A major problem with this new trend is the idea of ACTION! Simply thinking thoughts does not bring about tangible objects. Thinking starts the positive flow of energy. It is what we do with this thinking that determines what we receive.

Comfort is easier than change. Maybe this is why change is so challenging. This is a matter of personal choice. Think how hard it is to change yourself and some of your habits. This idea offers great insight on why we cannot change another individual. The only person you can change is YOU. Challenge yourself to become a unique individual that attracts whatever you desire in life. Take a long look at the negative, disgruntled individuals around you. Do not talk as they talk. Do not walk as they walk. Do not read what they read. Do not go where they go. Do not act as they act. Most importantly, become your own unique person and contribute to society in a positive way. Only the few have ever made the major life changes in this world. They stepped outside their box of fears. Become one of the few who have majored in the majors of life.

Majoring in majors often means simple action. A fishing colleague of mine, Terrance, once sat back on a cliff and watched a self-proclaimed expert angler in action. The object of this day was hooking large salmon or "big fish" as the locals call them. The angler was a veteran, and on this foggy morning, he hooked several large fish in short time. Finally, he landed and retained one. The angler then crossed the river to where my colleague was sitting.

A conversation broke out. "Can you please tell a fella a few tips on hooking those big fish?" Terrance asked, as he sat on the cliff.

The angler paused, looked him straight in the eyes and replied, "There is only one tip you need to know. You got to have your fly in the water." The angler walked on and Terrance got the message. We need to be "doing" in order to be "achieving". Many times we need to hear the truth, about ourselves before change can happen.

The truth about ourselves empowers us to change and to be free from past destructive behaviors. Personal development studies of the top successful people in the world taught me this. Observing how the super successful have attracted into their lives the unique qualities and quantities they possess is truly incredible. We must plan to look beyond formal schooling and into the major University of Life for the answers.

Be At Your Best

Ethics and proposed moral standards of conduct are not only professional, but also, personal. If individuals who lead a government or team organization are dishonest, we can be certain that it carries over into their personal lives. Those who use power and corruption also let these destructive forces carry over into other life areas. Who you are on the team is who you are in life. My cousin, Michael Hayter, told me this after my unique life changing story on the Pinware River. It was a mistake and he told me that who I was on the river is who I am in life. Thus, it was best to be in tip top health and decision-making shape at all times. It makes sense.

Skipper Bruce preached the "doing your best daily" philosophy to many people. In doing your best you cannot go wrong. Are you at your best on a daily basis? Now is the only moment you have so make the most of it. Why not put your ideas to work and do what you want in life? Be a leader not a follower. Learn to lead your own ship and steer it in a better life direction. These minor changes in major life areas will equal major future results.

Chapter 8 Nuggets for Digestion:

~ Formal education is not enough; we need self-education on a daily basis.
~ Formal schooling teaches people what to think.
~ Self-education teaches people how to think.
~ Do not die with your "music" still inside of you.
~ Now is the time to plan your new future.
~ A job is an economic necessity; a career is a love of life.
~ Learn to think outside the boxes of life.
~ Never let people box you in.
~ Do you feel boxed in today? If so, unpack that box!
~ The only boxes erected are the ones we construct.
~ Become a free thinker and practice higher order thinking.
~ Learn to attract better results by becoming a better person.
~ We cannot change another human being.
~ Learn how to work with the laws of life for better results.
~ Keep your fly in the water!
~ Be at your best daily!

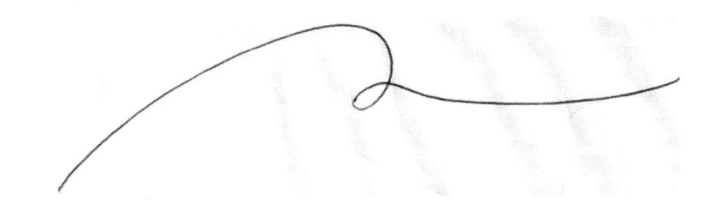

Rodney, Amber and Samantha are thinking outside the TV box.
Image © by <u>1st Site Web Design</u>

9

Health is Wealth and MUCH MORE!

The best things in life money cannot buy.
Skipper Michael Joseph Bruce

Skipper Bruce's wise words still ring loud in my ears: "Without health we do not have very much; your health is the most important thing in life." We all know of people who work hard on their jobs but not hard on their health. The philosophy of disease is work, work, and work, while simultaneously neglecting your health. The philosophy of life leadership success is balance; health first and all else next. Your own health and wellness is the greatest value you can bring to a relationship or to a company. Being healthy allows you to be more productive in all life areas, thus contributing in ways that make a difference in other people's lives. Skipper Bruce was correct, "Health is MAJOR!"

"The best things in life money cannot buy" was the second of three philosophical health phrases that Skipper Bruce practiced. We cannot put a price tag on a human life. How much is your arm worth? What about one of your eyes? Would you give one up for material wealth? Asking these questions makes us think about what really matters most in life.

"Take good care of yourself because your health, once gone, cannot be brought back" was his third nugget of wisdom. What simple, yet powerful, ideas! Many people waste valuable time on things, such as television, designed to divert our attention, relieve our interim pain, and take us away from the realities of life. If people exercised during this hour of television or used the extra hour for sleep, we can be certain that many of our minor ailments, such as lack of energy, would cease to exist.

Foundational Lifestyle

Our health affects everything else. Many times we fail to realize that we even have health unless something is wrong with it. Take nothing for granted. Seeing someone in a wheelchair, paralyzed from the waist down, makes me give thanks for the use of my legs. Everyone has his or her battles. Life would be easier, however, if we protected what we had and took our health seriously. People who have lost part of their health due to neglect, also have the same message: "Health is a treasure; I wish I had to make better decisions to keep mine." My fishing buddy, Bradley, who has lost the use of his kidneys, further solidifies Skipper Bruce's wisdom, "Your health is everything." Yes, our health does affect everything else and if we are to achieve well, we must feel well. For some of us, this means get well.

A healthy lifestyle, or style of living, involves simple choices that help to keep our health vibrant and strong. Some of these choices include a daily walk, daily nutritious meals, adequate sleep based on personal needs and, of course, drinking plenty of water. Human beings are approximately 70% water so we must keep the reservoir full for better daily bodily functions. Some other choices include refraining from smoking cigarettes or other substances and limiting or eliminating the use of alcohol. These are simple choices often requiring much self-discipline, especially when peer pressure or the need to fit in takes precedent over your health. Nothing must take precedent over your health. It is your body - the only place you have to live. Make better choices that keep you living well.

Sound Physical Health

Physical health is important. The human being is predominantly a mobile creature. Our whole body system is made to move. We need to keep moving. Being healthy involves quality, daily, physical activity. It does not take much to get started. Parking your car furthest from the door at the grocery store or taking the stairs instead of the elevator are simple starting points to becoming more active. Everything counts! Getting started is always the most difficult part of any life change. Once started on a daily physical activity plan, the process becomes easier and easier. The positive reinforcement allows us to keep going in a more productive fashion. So get moving!

Using the body allows it to remain limber and mobile. Not using it causes the body to deteriorate. Like the car engine that is not driven for a long time, the body will also stiffen and refuse to operate. Often, it is easier to get a new engine and repair the vehicle when it grinds to a halt. The human body, however, does not operate this way. Staying active is the preventive remedy - and solution. It sounds simple.

Many, however, have become conditioned to bad habits. The power to choose is the answer in this case. Choose to take your power back into your own hands and start today to work on improving your most important commodity, your health.

Obesity is prevalent in today's society. We see it in our young generation. Personal choice is the answer to fixing some of the obesity problems. The real culprit for obesity is lack of daily activity. People do not realize how easy change is! Decide to get moving and move! There is no other formula as simple. Start today on an activity program of your choice, beginning with the small simple steps, and progress from there. Walking is the best way to begin. It is the easiest exercise for most people. A walk a day, combined with the apple, will keep your medical team away! When the time is right and you are ready, you can progress to more intense activities and challenges. Having a friend who can share the activity program with you is one way to keep you active.

Relationships and Friends

Solid friends make the journey worthwhile. They also help us live well and can influence us in a positive direction when we have gone astray. Choose your friends wisely. We have all had to eliminate those wolves, dressed up like sheep, in our lives. This is normal. It is not going to change. Those two powerful words, "Be careful", from Skipper Bruce, when talking about safety and false friends, still remain fresh. Many friends have the potential to drain our energy, unknowingly…if we let them. Once again, it is up to us to make the better decisions. As Zig Ziglar says,

"Some people find fault like there is a reward for it." Do you have any false friends that need to be eliminated? Eliminating false friends can be challenging but it is essential for your better life future.

Having friends, with whom you may talk, who are non-judgmental and supportive, is therapeutic. To vent your frustrations and to share your feelings with another is lifelong learning at its finest. A burden shared is a lighter load. Not enough of us do this; yet, when we do, we feel much better. We will never have hundreds of close friends. We know who our real friends are. They are there for us unconditionally. It is always a give- and-take compromising relationship, not a "one way street". Develop and keep a solid group of close friends to make your journey much more enjoyable. Sometimes, however, as friends are often not trained in psychotherapy, professional counseling, which involves the art of active listening, is required.

Optimum Mental Health

When professional counseling is required, the short term intervention is the best approach. At the end of the day, it is all self-help, or personal development. The counselor helps clients to better help themselves. No one person can change another. Counselors provide a spark, a non-judgmental active listening ear to vent the issues and the tools to get well and stay well. It is up to the client to put the tools and approaches in action. Long term counseling intervention is big business for many therapists and the clients often remain dependent on the counselors for support. Whether or not you have a need for professional counseling, take your mental health in your own hands.

Without solid mental health, we cannot survive. Humans may be considered mental creatures, within a body to house our brains and nervous systems. We are different from animals in that we are able to think and make logical decisions. Skipper Bruce used his mental capacities to the fullest, thinking positive happy thoughts as much as possible. This was reflected in his overall attitude of optimism. His lesson "Live each day to the best of your ability with a happy attitude" was simple. Thinking positively is often a challenge in our society; but, it is a much better approach to overall health and vitality.

In visiting a poor country, I was amazed at how happy and content the citizens were. They were poor economically, but rich on the inside. Maybe it was because they did not understand western culture and they were not a part of our capitalist system. Material things cannot make us happy. Happiness, like health, is an inside job. I asked Skipper Bruce in his later years, "Can money buy happiness or make you happy?" His response was simple. "No, it can help, but it cannot buy you happiness." He went on further, "Money can only buy more and it just makes you more of what you already are." What a philosophy to live by! Wealth does not mean health but health is wealth. Mental health is powerful mental wealth.

Sound mental health involves keeping negative stress levels at a minimum. Stress is our greatest enemy. It may be considered the silent killer because it eats away subtly at our health and wellness. It can cause burn-out - on the job, in a relationship, at home, on a team. We must not underestimate the power of positive or negative stress. Preventing negative stress is a challenge. Sometimes this is hard to do in the environments where we place ourselves and in the conditions where we operate. Daily positive choices have the power to make or break us. We must choose them for overall body and mind nourishment. Meet the challenge!

The human brain is the most powerful mechanism on earth. It must be nourished. Many of us take for granted that it is always going to be there. The brain is our choice mechanism, allowing us to make better decisions, especially about our health and well being. Further, it is the decision maker that allows us, at any time, to choose a new career, a new relationship, or a new place in which to live. We must not take this for granted. How are you nourishing your mind? Reading books, debating controversial issues, listening to voices of value, such as Skipper Bruce, and watching educational programming are all means to mental health empowerment. Hanging out with people who will challenge you to be your best and taking in public seminars and activities where great ideas are shared are other ways to keep you sharp and mentally focused on your life leadership journey. Nourish your mind daily and allow it to affect others in a helpful way.

SAFETY!

Safety is a major aspect of staying healthy. From his past experiences before unions existed, Skipper Bruce spoke highly of this concept. On occasion, he observed some people making careless decisions on construction sites. His wisdom told me that life is too valuable about which to be casual. Safety is serious business.

Staying safe also involves personal decisions. Wearing your seat belt, not drinking and driving, not driving with someone who has been under the influence of chemicals, staying away from unattended construction sites and always educating yourself on the pros and cons of making a decision are ways of practicing safety. Lessons from the past teach us that life can disappear in the briefest moment of carelessness. We all know of someone who has experienced such a tragic event. Tragedies and accidents appear in the daily news. These people are often careless in their safety decision-making processes. Companies spend mega dollars on educating their employees and team members about safety concepts and procedures. It is always best to play safe.

I remember going to work for a factory freezer company that imported and exported seafood products. My father was working on the day of my first shift, so Skipper Bruce drove me to work. He was given a tour of the ship by a friend who worked for the company. On this day, Skipper Bruce advised, "Stay out of the hole", "Stay out of the hole", "Stay out of the hole while the crane is lowering or raising the pallet." He repeated this advice to me about 10 times. I knew the point he was making! Being a follower of his wisdom and knowledge, I listened carefully as he overemphasized the point of being safe and staying out of the hole.

Accidents happen. Skipper Bruce delivered a powerful message that sits well with me today. He said, "Don't be a hero for these guys; you're only another worker." He continued, "The only real hero is a live hero; a dead hero is no good." I got the message. A few years later, when I was in Ontario, the tragedy happened. A worker at the same plant did not get out of the hole and the apparatus broke. The pallet of frozen fish fell and killed him instantly. When I heard the news from my parents, I had wished that worker had heard my safety presentation from Skipper Bruce. Take no chances in high risk situations.

Preventing accidents from happening is simple foresight. A little preparation combined with caution and wisdom can go a long way. Why wait for your health to deteriorate and then take action? It is best to make the simple easy life choices and changes now, for a better tomorrow. This involves choosing to be safe and healthy, and doing whatever it takes to take care of you!

Foresight and Prevention

Many marriages fall apart and many relationships dissolve due to lack of foresight. The couple often courts each other in the beginning and, over time, the spark and "little things that make the big difference" disappear. When a relationship ends, the family members often comment "It just happened". It did not, however, just happen. A gradual process of neglect and carelessness over time allowed the healthy relationship to crumble.

Relationships are a major part of the health process. Life is stressful enough. A caring partner, at the other end of our relationship spectrum, must be there to support us, and not to take away from us. Preventing intimate relationships from disintegrating involves daily, quality decisions for the benefit of both parties. We need both foresight and hindsight as lifelong learning tools but, oftentimes, foresight is better than hindsight. Why wait for a disaster to happen?

No amount of money can buy your health back once it has deteriorated. Preventive medicine is the key to quality of life. At best, our health care system is a disease management system. Ample dollars are spent in crisis management. What we need most are better education, physical education and healthy active living initiatives. People are starting to catch on and the health movement is trying to lead the way. The "system" helps, but it is not enough for our own level of health, happiness and satisfaction. We must remember, however, that it is up to us to make it happen because only we can change who we are.

Many people now spend as much time as they can in nature - breathing fresh air, walking, and partaking in outside activities. Outdoor, healthy, active living has multiple benefits for the mind and body. As peace and solitude exist in nature, spending time outdoors is therapeutic. It allows you to reflect on how your life is working - therapy of the best kind. People from major cities all over the world enjoy a trip to Newfoundland and Labrador, Canada, to experience Mother Nature at her finest- the icebergs, landscape, ocean scenery, rivers and streams, untouched pristine environments and fresh air. Spend time in nature to discover who you really are and what you are all about. Being at one with nature helps keep us in top condition for the daily realities and stresses of life.

Fly-fishing has helped me to keep my physical and mental health. This carries over to life happiness. How can you worry and fly-fish at the same time? What is your passionate adventure for happiness that will also keep you healthy? Seek solitude and peace of mind daily. We all need as much of this as possible in a world of constant change. Meditation is also one way to keep you at peace. Find the ways and means to create internal peace.

Being at peace with yourself allows you to experience more joy in life. When there are little worries, your mind is free to do whatever it chooses. Inner peace is a healthy part of lifelong learning. Many people do not know how to be by themselves and enjoy life. Learning this is challenging, but rewarding in the long term. Choose and go do it!

Healthy Life Balance

Balance is the secret to life fulfillment. We all strive for it. On a minute by minute basis our physical bodies attempt to maintain internal balance or homeostasis. This ensures that the proper amount of vitamins, minerals, water, sugars, amino acids, fatty acids and life necessities are in order. When out of order, the body tries to regroup and does what is necessary to regain the proper delicate life balance.

In our own ways, we are striving for balance regularly. University students often stay up all night to finish a project or prepare for a test. When the body is out of balance, stress will sometimes set in and take its toll on health, happiness and well-being. We have all been there. We all need an adequate balance of work and play, family and friends, health and vitality, and of course, physical and mental health. Maintain balance in your health, relationships, and career. This prevents the body from having to deal with much unneeded stress. We must learn to balance the things that matter most.

Have a sound mind in a sound body. As the mind and body work together, synergy of both is important. Everything affects everything else in life. We have one body and one life to live. Who is the most important person reading this book now? You are! When you learn to take better care of yourself, you will ensure a healthy, happy future. As Skipper Bruce would say, "Absolutely!"

Chapter 9 Nuggets for Digestion:

~ Your health is the most important piece of your life.
~ You cannot put a realistic price tag on your health.
~ Health affects everything.
~ Take nothing for granted.
~ Make better health decisions.
~ Everything counts!
~ We are mobile creatures. Use it or lose it.
~ Choose your friends wisely.
~ Always, "Be Careful!"
~ A burden shared is a lighter load.
~ Be there for your friends unconditionally.
~ "There is no road to happiness; happiness is the road."
~ Health and happiness come from within.
~ Money only makes you **more** of what you already are.
~ Money cannot buy health and happiness; these must be chosen…daily!
~ Stress is our greatest enemy.
~ The only real hero is "a live hero".
~ Prevention is better than crisis management.
~ Spend time in nature, away from the hustles and bustles of daily living.
~ Seek peace of mind and solitude.
~ Practice healthy **balance** in your day-to-day living.

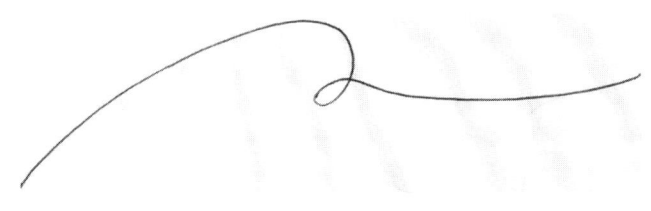

10

Onward We Sail

Help each other out; it's what life is really all about.
Skipper Michael Joseph Bruce

The future is where we are going and the past is where we have been. The past is a school of education for each of us. In counseling we often teach clients to write their own obituaries. If they do not like what they write, they know that now is the time to change it! Do you ever stop and wonder what will be said about you when you pass away? Pondering this question, we can learn to slow down from our fast-paced ways to appreciate the people that are here with us now. Keep going forward into the future; there is no other way.

The people who help shape us are powerful pieces in our life puzzle and remembering the deceased in a healthy way helps keep us focused on what really matters most. The people we lose can be ever remembered. I can still see Skipper Bruce, with tears in his eyes, as he visited his parents at the graveside in Long Harbor, Placentia Bay, Newfoundland. While it is healthy to remember those who have helped shape us, life goes on. Move on with it.

We must remember that life really is about people. It would be a lonely life if we did not have people to work with, struggle with, talk with, laugh with and cry with. Who are the most important people in your life? Have you put them aside in quest for "things" of lesser value? As time passes quickly use it to focus on our fellow human beings.

Spending Time

Spend your time wisely. Lloyd Colbourne from the previous local Nature show, *Newfoundland Outdoors* once commented, "Life really is short, but every day is a good day so make the most of it." Skipper Bruce agreed. We cannot change the weather or what happens, but we can change ourselves. Why not use your time to make the most of the life you have to live?

The clock is ticking. As we get older, it seems that time goes by faster. As a child I, like you, remember waiting for the summer to arrive. School was over and playing softball had taken its place. Waiting for summer seemed like forever! Time had no end. Time, however, stops for no one. Mother advised, "Never put off until tomorrow what you can do today. There is no time like the present". We call it time management; however we spend time, not manage it. We all have one life to live - one chance to perform here on earth. Make the most of it!

What is your reality? The fundamental ideas presented here have worked and continue to work for many people. Of course, they are up for debate as real education allows us to see multiple points of view. This book is one point of view, written at one moment in time. The only truth we know is our own truth. We can all learn and review the fundamental ideas that often get overlooked or forgotten in daily living.

Spending time going back to basics will keep us moving onward in a productive way.

To The Fullest

How do we live life to the fullest? Discover your unique potential. While talent comes from within, human behavior is learned. Learned behavior can also be unlearned. Nothing is more horrible than being stuck in a career, in a relationship or in a life situation that you do not enjoy. Making better decisions and following others who have succeeded help us to move forward.

Your own unique creativity is the key element in designing the life you wish to live. No one has your specific creative inborn talents. Develop these now and put them to work. Even though we must work in order to survive, life was designed for us to enjoy. Why not enjoy it? Many people do not live to their full potential. The greatest stories may never be told. The greatest talents may never be developed. Skipper Bruce advised, "Do your best always and know that you have done your best no matter what". What simple, yet influential, words by which to live!

Talent and genius cannot be denied. To help you find your own unique life niche, work on you and your talents. Krista, a friend of mine says, "I'm not like other people". She prefers being who she is. Practice and celebrate being unique. Celebrate being you.

Who Really Cares!

My buddy, Wayne Hanlon, *The Fishing Magician*, enjoys the outdoors. He rarely cares what others think about his love of sports fishing. Be it early morning, late evening, mid afternoon, when Wayne decides to go fishing, he goes. He does not let anything, or anyone, keep him away from his time for peace and solitude. Wayne will often bring home a catch, when many will not, and share it unselfishly with his friends. If only more of us had this unselfish attitude, while at the same time not caring what others think.

Many people struggle with feelings of inferiority. Helping people believe that they are equal can be difficult. In my teenage years, I remember not liking my name. I was wishing I was someone else and I wanted to change my name to be more popular with the "in crowd". Have you ever experienced this feeling? In puberty, we search for our own identities. It takes time, patience and life experience to grow and learn that we are who we are and that we are OK! Skipper Bruce often stated, "Who really cares what other people think?" He did not mean this in a selfish way. He meant it for real life purpose.

Your future depends on what you think matters. Ignore the gossip and jealousy of other people. When you walk into a room full of people, everyone has a different opinion about you. None of these opinions **are** you. Denis Waitley says it best:

Motives and fears run deep. Study them in others. The sympathetic fair-weather friend, who supports you and comforts you when you're down, may like you best when you are in just that state: down and dependent.

Go forth with your mental filter on high. Negative people and energy suckers exist, waiting for their opportunity to chip away at your achievements and self-esteem. Expect this to happen. It is part of life. Acceptance is powerful. It was life-changing for me and it can be life-changing for you. Once I accepted that I could not change anyone but me, things seemed to change. In reality, life was just going on as usual. I was the one who changed. Often reading a book the second time gives us new insight. The book did not change. We changed!

One idea of acceptance is that business people do care. They are no different than anyone else, all searching for something, including love and more of the next life experience. Just because they have more "things" does not make business people better or worse. Many of us think negative about people who are rich and possess worldly treasures. The majority of these people work extremely hard at what they do. Accept people for who they are and not what they do. This opens our channels for greater things to come. What things must you accept in order to better move forward on your life leadership journey?

Giving Thanks

Skipper Bruce always gave thanks, for everything. Be it a meal, day fishing, a visit from a relative or just an ordinary day where he was able to go and help out in the community,

Skipper Bruce gave thanks. He knew that being thankful for what he had, opened the channel for more to flow in. Now is the time for us all to give thanks. Life does get better when we learn to give thanks. An "attitude of gratitude" will make our lives more enjoyable.

University of Life

"Go to work harder on yourself than on anything else", as Jim Rohn suggests. The simple philosophy of Personal Development is that life gets better when we get better. Education, combined with action, are fundamental to a new you. Many avenues of education exist. The greatest is your own personal development and lifelong learning program. Life is really all about you. There is no telling what is possible when we put our goals and dreams to work. Study the lessons of other successful people and follow in their footsteps. Stand on the shoulders of winners.

Skipper Bruce told me one summer while I worked on a construction site in Ontario, "You'll learn an awful lot there." He meant the valuable lessons of dealing with life and with people are found on such job sites. He was correct. The University of Life is where we "walk our talk". Seriously consider Skipper Bruce's unique philosophies and ideas. Then do what you must do to live your life to the fullest. Make a choice to take the "road less traveled" because it does make all the difference in your final result. What is best for you is what you decide. When you go to work on your talents and skills, they will go to work for you.

As I have discovered, when the student is ready, the teacher mysteriously appears. I hope this book will act as your teacher, with silent mentor Skipper Bruce helping you lead your own ship. Remain a student of life, accepting the fact that there really are no experts. You, and only you, know what is best for you.

Altruistic Love

We must accept ourselves for who we really are, not just what we do. The personal development quest is often painful. Digging to the bottom of your heart and healing the bruises that are there is necessary for a better future. Learn to be calm, peaceful and more relaxed.

In the midst of everyday living, we all seek love. It is the greatest virtue and answer to all of life's hurts. We cannot give to another that which we do not possess ourselves. You cannot give me five dollars if you do not possess it. The same holds true for love. Unless our own love tanks are filled, we cannot give any away. We must remember this important idea. Self-love is the greatest love of all and without it, we cannot receive. Giving starts the receiving process. Skipper Bruce not only preached it, he lived it…daily. We must learn to live it as well. Learn to love yourself first and all else will come your way.

I remember this lesson as if it were yesterday when Skipper Bruce took me to one of his favorite "secret" trouting spots. On this day, we fed chicken to the trout as they breached around us. This day was significant for me as I, at the young age of eight, caught more than he did. As Skipper Bruce prepared the meal, I fished some more. He was preparing for my greatest lesson. Finally it was time to eat and he had his words crafted perfectly in the form of a question. Great teachers always ask questions because the person asking questions controls the conversation.

He began, "Little Paul, (as I was called back then by family and close friends) if a young native woman came by with her child and they were hungry and we had all of this food, what would you do?" I was speechless. He repeated the question a few minutes later as I sat and looked at our buffet spread, fit for two kings - which we were. Skipper Bruce had my attention.

I started in on my scrumptious ham sandwich that Nan had made for me that morning. He asked me the question again, for a third time, with the following addition, "If they were very hungry and did not have any food to eat, what would you do?" I was stuck for words but realized something major was about to transpire. I asked, "What would you do, Poppy Bruce?" He replied skillfully without hesitation, "I would share what we have with the lady and her child. They are in need and I would help them out." I got the message loud and clear. Skipper Bruce continued, "Sharing is what life is really all about." Sharing does make room for more and helping people out is what makes life worthwhile.

The journey keeps going forward. You must keep going forward on it. Become like the schooner that cannot go backwards. "Hoist your main, trim your sail, look straight ahead, and keep on going." Finally, gather wisdom as you sail and not only learn from it, but share it with others as well, so that they may learn. Share ideas to help other people better lead their ships. Share what you have because you are a better person than you used to be. Sharing is the ultimate essence of life. Absolutely!

Chapter 10 Nuggets for Digestion:

~ The future is where we are going.
~ Write your own obituary and change now to make it what you want!
~ Remember the deceased who have taught us well.
~ Life is really about people.
~ Every day is a great day; make the most of each and every one.
~ Never put off until tomorrow what can be done today.
~ Go back to the basics when necessary; keep life simple.
~ Discover your own unique potential and do what you want to do.
~ It is your life to live!
~ Talent and genius cannot be denied.
~ When you put your talents to work, they will put you to better work.
~ Who cares what others think, do what you must do anyway!
~ What other people think about you is none of your business.
~ Accept life on life's terms.
~ Accept you for who you really are – an excellent person.
~ "Stand on the shoulders of giants" and learn from others who have gone before.
~ Take the "road less traveled" and create the life you desire.
~ Work harder on yourself than on anything else.
~ Remain a student for life, ever learning about people and life.
~ Learn to be calm and peaceful, daily.
~ Love is the answer we are all searching for; it comes in strange packages.

~ We cannot give that which we do not have.
~ Giving always starts the receiving process in a healthy relationship.
~ Develop the gratitude attitude. Always give thanks for what you already have.
~ The show must go on, so we must also go on.
~ Share ideas and education to help people on their life ships.
~ You set the sail on your life ship, so set it wisely and adjust where necessary.

Twenty years from now you will be more disappointed by the things that you didn't do than by the ones you did do. So throw off the bowlines. Sail away from the safe harbor. Catch the trade winds in your sails. Explore. Dream. Discover.
Mark Twain

Concluding Story

Charmed and Ready for Action!

The real university is the University of Life! Always remain a student. Keep learning, stay healthy, keep reading and be a collector of SOLID IDEAS that you put to work for you. This educational approach will take you to places you never dreamed possible!
Paul Michael White

It was late evening and the sun was setting fast. The place was southern Labrador's Pinware River, an Atlantic salmon angler's dream. My good buddy, Morris Lynch, and I had spent the last week fishing this mighty river and we enjoyed plenty of action. I had already hooked and released a 12-pound beauty at Guy's Point, retained one for "Mudder" and lost several more in the process. Morris had his quota of two retained and was now in the catch and release mode. He rose five large salmon up to this point, two of which came on the same cast for a deadly dry fly pattern he calls "the Dirt Fly." Our goal on this late evening was for me to retain my final fish.

We had less than two hours of quality fishing time before the sun set. Morris and I headed for Buckle's Point, my favorite stretch on the river. The morning before, I retained my first grilse of the season there. The river was high and the fish were moving fast. When we arrived at the main rock, Morris had the game plan for action: "I'll fish here and you go down to where you got the fish yesterday. Stay within an earshot and if you hear me whistle, it means I rose one; come up and have a smack at 'im'."

Morris and his veteran fishing buddies from the Placentia area have used this buddy system technique for many years. When someone has his quota he unselfishly gives a buddy a chance at hooking one. All he does is pull the fly away on the rise and let another angler have a cast in hopes of hooking the interested salmon. It may pay off in times when other anglers are having luck and you are not. "Treat others the way you would like to be treated" is a good motto to live by. I learned that one in the Boy Scouts where I first met Morris several years ago when he and Dad were Scout leaders.

Away I went to the "lie" where I hooked a fish the day before. Apparently it is only a good lie in high water though, because of the way the river bends around a series of rocks. I was not halfway down to my spot and had not even wet a fly, when I heard a whistle. I bolted up the river like lightning. When I got to the main rock, I discovered that Morris had lost a fish. He did not whistle the first time because he thought it was a large trout. Having lost this one, he flicked out again and rose another in the middle of the pool. This time, to give me a chance, he pulled away before the fish inhaled the fly. Morris lost the first fish on a Blue Charm and rose the second one on the same fly. It was a deadly pattern, very dark with thick silver ribbing and cream colored moose hair for the wing.

Having tried my "Pinware Special" fly to no avail and not wanting to waste another minute, I said to Morris, "Lend me your rod." It had the deadly Blue Charm, which initially enticed the fish, attached to it. His rod was a $600 Fenwick *Ironfeather* which had been replaced twice after Morris had broken it on the Pinware River playing out fish. I took the rod, which was heavier than mine with the reel on the opposite side, and cast to the spot where he rose the fish. After eight or 10 casts, it was evident the fish was either not interested, or more likely, had moved on. I handed Morris back his rod and headed downstream to my spot once again.

I had only walked about 100 feet down the river when I heard his shrieking whistle. I turned and headed back to the pool, which we later realized, was full of fish. Morris rose another on his dark Blue Charm variation. I did not hesitate to try again and, before I had the words "Lend me your rod" out of my mouth, Morris had placed the Fenwick Battlestick in my hand and I was into my first cast. The fish made a swirl but missed the fly. I cast back a few more times. No luck. Morris, acting as my guide, said, "Strip off more line. He's lying in the tail end and seems to be following the fly across the pool." I did as he suggested, made a few false casts and flicked my fly far to the other side where the fast current swept it to the salmon's lie. I could only see my bright line in the water as the fly traveled behind its graceful swing.

Morris yelled, "You got "im!" I failed to lift in time, however, because I did not see the fish take it. When I did lift, a few seconds later, I felt the line tighten, but the fish spit the hook before I set it. The long line traveled towards me and I let it straighten out on the back-cast before powering it forward. As the line straightened, we heard a "snap" as the fly smacked a large boulder behind us. Blue Charm No 1 was gone!

"You got another fly like that one?" I asked Morris. He searched through his fly boxes. He rarely loses a fly. Morris tied on the fly with a hitch behind the head once again and I grabbed the rod, flicked out and rose a fish. I cast to the tail end of the pool and rose another. Like the previous one, this fish did not return. Just as I had given up, I flicked out and was handing the rod back to "Guide Lynch" while the current carried the fly. As Morris was taking the rod out of my hands, a nice fish rose to "our" fly. Amazing! Two anglers rising the same fish, at the same time, on the same rod!

Morris hauled the fly away and gave me the rod. We looked at each other dumbfounded and laughed. I made several casts but the fish did not return. Morris took the rod and made one cast to the far end of the pool. A large fish churned the water as the fly "skittered" across the lip of the pool and the veteran angler pulled away with perfect timing. Now he had it figured out - the fish were lying in the far end of the pool to the left. They were following the fly into the shallow water where they would try to take it.

I flicked the fly to the far side and, as it traveled across, a fish grabbed it with a sweeping curl. The hook was set on impact. It was a nice fish, about 10 pounds. He jumped several times and I knew he was over the 63-cm limit and would have to be released.

As I tried to jump to the large rock on shore from the smaller one on which I was standing, I held the fish tight. The salmon made one springing leap and broke the leader. Blue Charm No 2 was gone! "You had him barred," Morris said, explaining how he saw a large ball of line dangling from my hand where I held onto the rod. I was playing him hard. When I tried to jump ashore from the rock, the line was held tight instead of playing the fish from the reel.

"You got any more Blue Charms?" Morris asked as we tried to figure out what had just happened. I then tied on one of my Blue Charms, with a half-hitch knot behind the head.
Meanwhile, Morris was crawling around behind me, searching for his first Blue Charm. It was getting dark and the fish could barely see the fly on the water, so Morris gave up looking and came back down to where I was standing. After several casts, he said he couldn't see my fly and wondered if I had the hitch tied properly. "Sure do," I replied.

He took a closer look and noticed the fly traveling about two feet from the fly line! The fish had broken the leader at the 10/12 pound test junction. I, in the dim light, just grabbed the end of the leader, figuring there was still plenty left, and tied on a new fly. Everything was happening so fast, I did not even check to see how close my fly was to the fly line!

"What have you got on there?" he asked, "A jigger leader?" The fly was hitched alright, but it was not attached to a nine-foot leader like the first two were! I had not realized it. I was losing his gear faster than we were rising fish! "Ya got me reamed out," Morris uttered as I flicked out and rose another fish. It was growing darker, so I had one more cast and, sure enough, rose another salmon close to the large rock. He never grabbed the fly, either, so we headed back to our trailer, laughing like we were just leaving a Yuk-Yuk's concert with Jim Carrey. "What happened just then?" I managed to ask through laughter. He replied, "We were doing pretty good 'til you went wild there at the end of it. And here I was like a fool, crawling around, looking for the first fly up in the rocks!"

That was my first trip to the Pinware River. As you've probably guessed, it will not be my last. Next time, though, I'll be prepared with my own rod and plenty of Blue Charms. If you ever hear someone whistle sharply on the Pinware River, Labrador, Canada go check out the action. It will be worth the entertainment and you may be in for quite a show! And if Morris decides to give you a smack at a fish he rose, be sure to have your own fly rod, "Charmed" and ready for action.

On your life leadership journey into the future, take a variety of great ideas and share them to help others. The thrill, and meaning of it all, is really in the hunt and not in the kill; in the fishing, not in the catch. May you find what you are fishing for and much, much more. Most importantly, have your own life "Charmed" and ready for action.

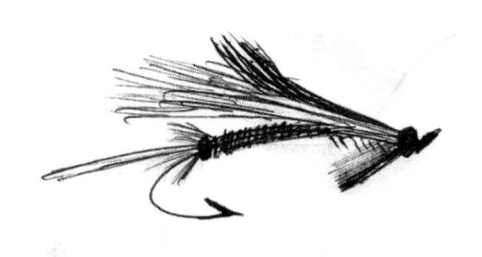

Acknowledgements

A very special acknowledgement goes to my parents for bringing me into this world and for helping me along the way. To Mom, baker and cook extraordinaire, the bird-watching guru and genius of the family, thank you from the bottom of my heart, for everything. To Dad, the greatest lead-guitarist and musician most of the world has not yet seen and the scrabble playing champ who I enjoy fishing with the most, thank you. Thank you both one more time for the many summer holiday adventures across our province, even though we never got a taste of salmon. Although up for debate, it never really was about the fish anyway.

A very sincere thank you to Joan M. Howard, my past high school English teacher and Literature Leader who has been my editor and helped make this project possible. Growing up next door to you and learning from you have been rewarding experiences; now it is time for your book Joan!

To Aunt Joanie Bruce, who has taught me so much along this journey, a very special thank you is extended. Wayne Dyer is right: "We teach people how to treat us."

Nanny White: thanks for the feeds, the chats, and for brightening my day each time I go to visit. May you live to see your 100th birthday!

Uncle Bill Hayter thanks for that inspiring conversation in Ottawa about using my energy to help people in ways I could not see at the time; now I understand.

Thank you to Darcy Ward and Bim Bridle for your final comments and input. Everyone must go to Red Bay, Labrador, and visit Whaler's Restaurant!

Thank you to Lorna Walters, Seanna Maher, Charles Cheeseman, Tina Hunt, Snow-PAL and all the "positive gang" for all of your help and constant daily encouragement. I cannot thank you enough. As Ringo Star sings, in a song wrote for him by Lennon and McCartney, "I get by with a little help from my friends." Friends like you make life worthwhile, THANKS!

Thank you Dr. Tony Simmonds for urging me into the field of Counseling Psychology, and for all those inspirational "Personality" classes back in University. When the other classes were stressful, your class **always** made my day and gave meaning to the life challenge. Rest in Peace Tony, and I am not a fan of hook and release either.

Anna-Lisa Varano, my dear friend in Ontario, thanks again for those powerful words "Only one life to live, Whitey, live it out loud!" You are a world winner Varano.

Thank you Christine Dowler for helping me push through my tough battles in Ontario, Canada at a time when I was lost and searching. You are truly a life saver, C. Thanks for helping me find, and help, myself.

Thanks to Krista Koerner for your wise words, especially "You can do **anything** you put your mind to Mr. White." I now really believe this, thanks so much Ms. K.

To Wayne Dyer, Denis Waitley, and Jim Rohn, THANK YOU for picking up where Skipper Mike Bruce left off and for helping me better myself to help people as best I can. You are THE three greatest Personal Development Leaders of all time.

Michael "Saunter" Howard, you are one of a kind. Thanks for showing up at a time in life when I had to delete some fair-weather friends and find real ones. They say things happen for a reason and I now believe this. It is always a pleasure to be around your wisdom and intuition. Sammy rules the feline kingdom! Keep your sail trimmed, Saunter, and always watch your bobber.

And finally, a very special thank you to Sharon *PianoBea* Clarke for "dropping by" at the right time in my life and teaching me so much more about myself, about human nature, about real intention and about the things I needed to learn at this time. As Zig Ziglar would say, "See you at the TOP!"

    p.s. You really are The BEST *Sharona*. Never forget that ... "In this life".

How do YOU see YOUR life catch?!

Image © by 1st Site Web Design

About the Author

Sharing life-helping ideas is what Paul Michael White does best. He is an Educational & Inspirational Speaker, Mental Health Counselor and Corporate Trainer who speaks regularly on the topics of Life Leadership, Health & Wellness, Personal Development and Self-Mastery. As a proud member of the Canadian Association of Professional Speakers (CAPS) and the Newfoundland and Labrador Association of Professional Speakers (NLAPS), he travels across Canada helping people improve their jobs and their lives, one choice at a time. Guided by a Masters Degree in Counseling Psychology, Paul loves the challenge of helping people help themselves – "We are all CEO's of our own companies." He is a dedicated member of Toastmasters International as well as a Certified Canadian Counselor.

Please see his website www.paulwhite.ca for more details and to reserve Paul as your next Professional Speaker!

email: info@paulwhite.ca

call: 1-709-687-1031

You are who you were,

up until now…